DESTINATIONS

JEAN-LOUIS DENIOT

DESTINATIONS
JEAN-LOUIS DENIOT

By PAMELA GOLBIN

Photography: Stephan Julliard / Christoph Theurer / Jonny Valiant / Anita Calero / Anouar Akrouh / Xavier Bejot / Richard Powers / Hunter Kerhart
Cover: Peter Rodger
Portraits: Sophie Delaporte

Art Direction by Paul McKevitt, Subtitleny

RIZZOLI NEW YORK

New York · Paris · London · Milan

Left: photography by Sophie Delaporte

CONTENTS

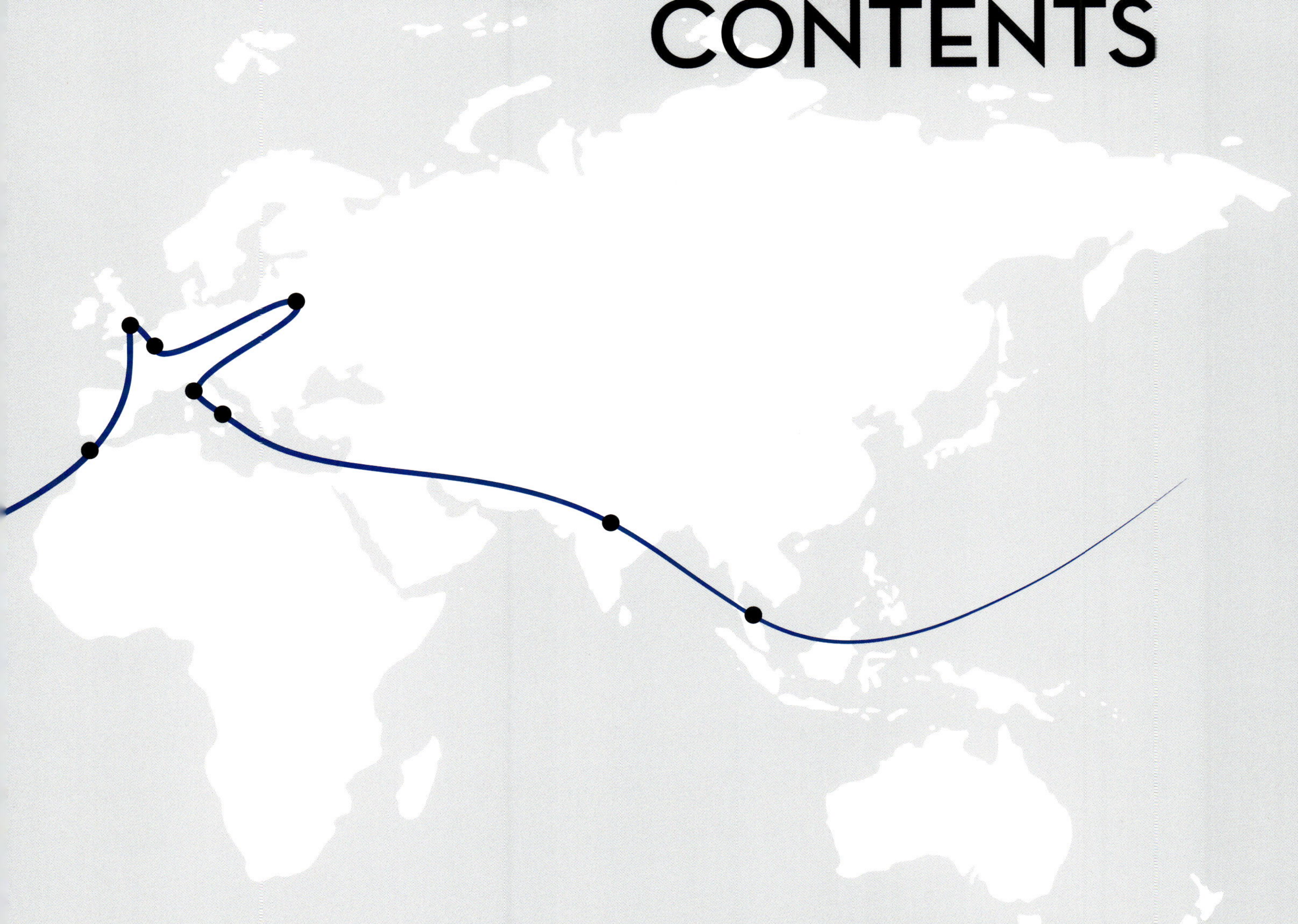

INTRODUCTION

BY PAMELA GOLBIN

Your mission statement sets the tone, "Design your life and dreams."

There are very few things you can control in life, but one thing you can do is design it and, by extension, the dreams will follow. It's all very connected, and at the end of the day it's all about emotions—how to channel them and how to create them in each surrounding space.

With this book you are taking the reader around the world to eighteen different destinations!

Penthouse apartments, townhouses, mid-century homes, sprawling villas, custom constructions, eighteen projects that each reflect a different aspect of my work. They are time capsules that bring together the past, present, and future through a surprising mix of antique and contemporary components that all take into consideration the particularities of each location. They surprise in their variety but they all have a common thread—passion.

You create seamless stories.

Yes, that everyone can appropriate. As a storyteller, I develop an entire setting, like a movie screenplay, to tell the best narrative I can out of an existing space. As soon as you open the entrance door, you are guided by a visual and physical story that is developed throughout to create a unified environment.

I begin with the bare piece of real estate that the client shows me as a layout. Then, I look for the flaws, the imperfections, the constraints. All the unsexy details that no one sees but that make all the difference. Those are the elements on which I spend the most time. My challenge is to make every room be the nicest room of the house by turning flaws and defects into surprising qualities.

Photography by Stephan Julliard

What is the most important element of each project?

My priority is always the person who will actually live in the homes I design. When will they be using the space? Do they lead a public or private life? What are their needs? I want to make them dream, to transport them, their friends, and family. My designs are tools for exaltation.

There are so many great architectural designs that are like contemporary sculptures. They are stunning, but once you put the human inside you realize there is rarely a dialogue between the two. For me, the design exists to serve the person not vice versa.

When you walk into a space, what is the first thing that immediately attracts you?

The view, always, always, always the view. When you like to play with perspectives, which I love to do, the view is the greatest perspective you can have. By pulling it inside, you extend the space, creating a continuity with the outside environment.

Would you say most of your work is in the art of being invisible?

Yes, absolutely. The large part of my work can't be seen because it's structural. If the skeleton is well thought out, the rest follows. My greatest compliment is when a space feels so natural it's as if it has always been this way. Then, you need to actually amplify it and create the rhythm, making different rooms stronger architecturally or decoratively depending on the flow from one space to another. The decoration can come and go because it doesn't have a sense of permanence. Once I'm finished with the architecture, the rest is like makeup.

In interiors, I find it interesting that only the human body can give it scale. Otherwise, you don't know if a sofa is three or nine feet long. It's by putting a human being in the context that you give scale to the space.

You attach great importance to lighting . . .

Lighting is the magical element that brings everything together. It's part of the layering that generates the overall atmosphere. You can hide or emphasize specific areas giving coherence, depth, and density to emphasize the elements that together create the perfect ambiance for every situation. It's like sculpting again.

Photographies by Stephan Julliard

Is it always about the real estate?

Yes, absolutely. First you have to start by doing justice to the piece of real estate. I think that's what I love the most: saving houses and apartments. I always have the impression that with architectural integrity comes a sense of serenity. A good house can be a studio or a ten-bedroom home. Each place comes with its own story. When I discover a house, it's like meeting a person for the first time.

There are two figures that had a big impact on your work: Henri Samuel and Alberto Pinto.

Diane de Beauvau introduced me to the prestigious Henri Samuel. At the time, I was in a situation to listen more than to participate and I was very discreet, captivated by his experiences. Samuel was known for a variety of great French styles, but I remember his grand salon on the rue du Faubourg Saint-Honoré with its striking red-orange upholstered walls that made the gold-on-white Empire woodwork just pop. It was a fabulous backdrop to Balthus's *Le Fruit d'or* and the experimental furniture, commissioned from contemporary artists such as César, Guy de Rougemont, and Philippe Hiquily. It showed me the importance of mixing classicism and the avant-garde to create an eclectic framework representing many periods and cultures. Using a much broader and enriched vocabulary has allowed me to create more interactions between objects, giving depth and scope to my storytelling.

I was also fascinated by Alberto Pinto because of all the locations where he worked. He was able to bring his talent to so many distant capitals and still keep the great fundamentals, always giving them a different shape, a singular perfume, or a distinctive color so as to be in perfect context with the locality. Very early on in my career, I made it a personal challenge to work in as many locations as possible, to constantly test my design, technical knowledge, and even personal comfort; to be able to adapt to each site so I could make my design happen. Today, I have projects on five different continents.

With Paris as your center . . .

Absolutely. Paris demands your best at all times, constantly pushing your limits and keeping you on your feet. Because of its celebrated history in the decorative arts, Paris dictates longevity. To leave a mark, you have to withstand the test of time.

Photographies by Stephan Julliard

PARIS
QUAI D'ORSAY

On Paris's Left Bank, at the intersections of the grand Esplanade des Invalides and the opulent Pont Alexandre III, the new headquarters of Jean-Louis Deniot are located front and center of the Seine River on the famed Quai d'Orsay. Deniot's creative hub, it is here where all of the projects are conceived, designed and elaborated by his team of thirty collaborators specializing in architecture, interior design, and custom furniture design.

How does it feel to be in your new offices?

I've spent most of my professional life in Paris physically moving closer to the river, one address at a time. It seems quite logical for me to have ended up on the Quai d'Orsay. And now that I am here, it's pure magic.

For the last eight years I had been looking for new offices that brought together an ideal space for my team with the perfect emblematic address. A dear friend once told me, "A good purchase always hurts." I agree because it's made out of sacrifices, doubts, and projection. Even though the renovations, the move, and the opening of the offices were particularly challenging due to the successive Covid lockdowns, it's worked out beautifully and perfectly positions us to embrace the future in the best possible conditions.

Photography by Stephan Julliard

A serendipitous event reassured you were on the right path, that it was all meant to be...

The renowned decorator Charles Sevigny lived in this building as did the couturier, Hubert de Givenchy, for whom Charles designed his apartment. Charles spent the latter part of his life at his storied house Dar Zero in Tangier, where we met and became friends. For my 40th birthday he gave me his personal architect table, which I brought out of storage to place in my new office. Flipping through a magazine, I saw a story on Charles's 100th anniversary celebration that included

a picture of him sitting at the same table at this exact address, just one floor up. It gave me such a feeling of relief knowing that it had come full circle. I feel, without a doubt, that this is the place where I am supposed to be.

The views play a central role in the layout design.

The spectacular views are the undisputable stars of this space. They open up uninterrupted perspectives to the water while generously filling the offices with natural light. The floor plan was created along an enfilade of floor-to-ceiling double windows that still have their original bronze

tinted frames, which give a lavish industrial feel to the place. I played with glossy ceilings and reflective floors to amplify the views and the sense of height. Instead of being contained in one single frame, the multifaceted views bounce throughout and give a sense of floating theatricality.

What was your approach for this space?

I wanted to treat it as an office even though it's the only commercial floor in a residential building. I placed a front desk when you walk in to make it clear that you're not in an apartment. It was all about creating a great sense of movement and bringing the comfort of home into the office environment since that's where we spend so much of our time. Whereas my previous offices were on street level in a house-like configuration, with a courtyard and a glass roof that diffused indirect

light to each inward-facing room, the new space is quite the opposite. Its countless large windows flood the interior with natural light and open the workspace outward into the cityscape. At night, the City of Light does not disappoint thanks to the luminescence of the street lamps that project their shine inside.

From where did the furniture come?

Most of the furniture came from my previous location. People get rid of things too quickly and too easily. On the contrary, I encourage people to collect and keep objects, which is why it was important for me bring them to this location. They created an instant feeling of stability and continuity with the past and brought an ease to our new environment.

It's the start of a new chapter.

It's like a reboot. It's very fresh, very inspiring. I founded my company in 2000 and now feel I have the perfect team, the perfect tools, and exciting projects all around the world. I am always eager to travel, to go to as many places as possible, to be able to perform in each one and then come home to this beautiful city.

High-gloss lacquered walls

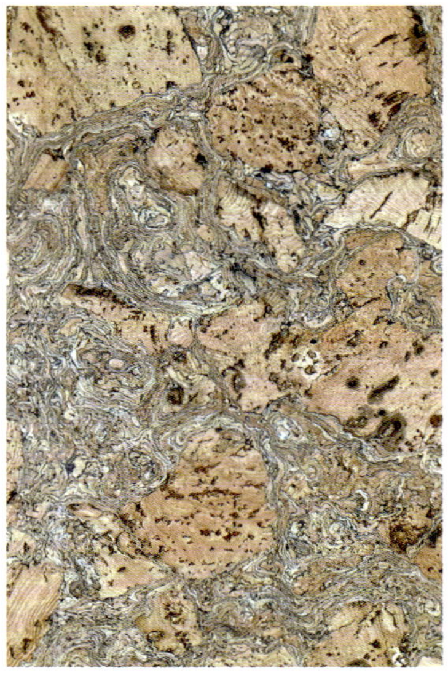
Cork

Casted concrete walls

Custom-designed JLD office table

Brushed granite

Wood veneer by Sotsass

PHOTO 1 / Desk custom designed by Jean-Louis Deniot / Table lamp "Bay" by Ettore Sottsass / Pair of wall lamp by Roll & Hill / Striped wallpaper by Lincrusta / Set of four 1940s chairs covered in Bisson Bruneel / Bronze console by Ado Chale / Table lamp "Baghdad" by Mathieu Matégot • **PHOTOS 2 & 3** / Wallpaper by Casamance / Chair by Ettore Sottsass / Grey sandstone console by Angelo Mangiarotti / Bronze seventeenth-century Ottoman candlestick / Sixteenth-century gold-carved wooden bust / Gold bronze table lamp by Michel Armand / Lithograph by Hans Hartung / Bronze wall lamp by Felix Agostini • **PHOTO 4** / Coffee table by Ado Chale / Custom-designed JLD sofa upholstered in Edmond Petit and Pierre Frey / Cushion in Boussac, Houlès piping / Adnet pair of floor lamps, lampshade by Anne Sokolsky / Abstract painting "Campagne" by Françoise Brunet / Empire porcelain *rafraichisseur* / Pair of seventeenth-century Spanish bronze candlesticks / 1930s bronze sculpture *Plateau au Trésor* / Pair of Piet Hein Eek armchairs / Side table by Hilquily from Yves Gastou / Drinks table by Cesare Lacca / Stoneware vase by Denbas / Flag by Sol LeWitt / Pair of fireside chairs "Pagoda" by Steiner Gilbert / Floor Lamp by Sciolari / Art déco golden column / Decorative marble ball by ME • **PHOTO 5** / Desk by Quinet / Xstool custom designed by JLD for Pouenat with Kirkby Design / 1930s industrial metal desk lamp / Porcelain bust of Junon / Pair of candlesticks by Hervé Van Der Straeten • **PHOTO 6** / Pair of mid-century chests of drawers by Gio Ponti / Pair of vintage table lamps / Pair of Art Déco ceramic ball vases / Pair of Louis XVI golden wood armchairs signed Louis-Charles Carpentier • **PHOTO 7** /

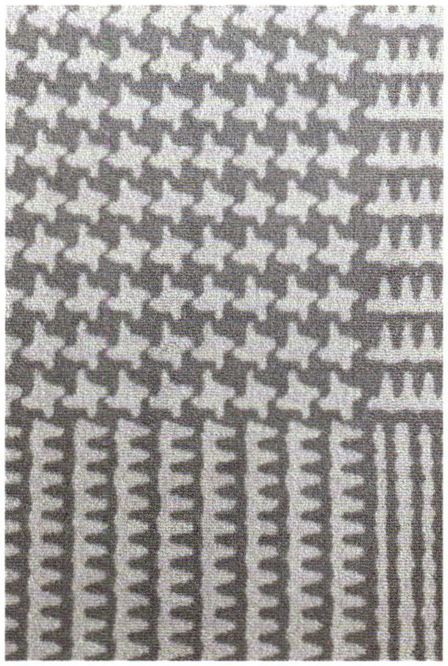
Custom-designed JLD wall-to-wall carpet

Wallpaper by Casamance

Versailles parquet

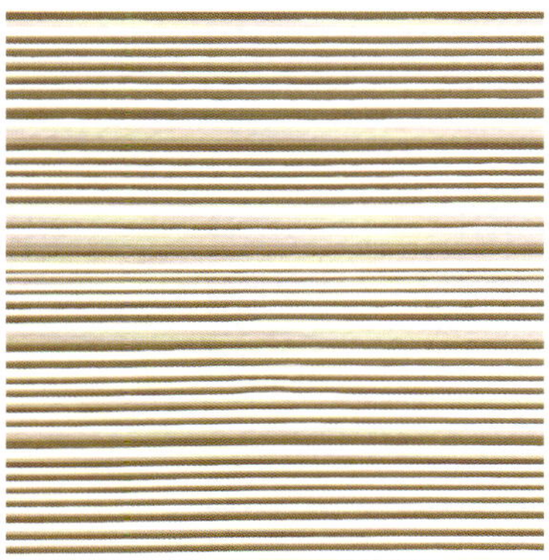
Paintable wallpaper by Lincrusta

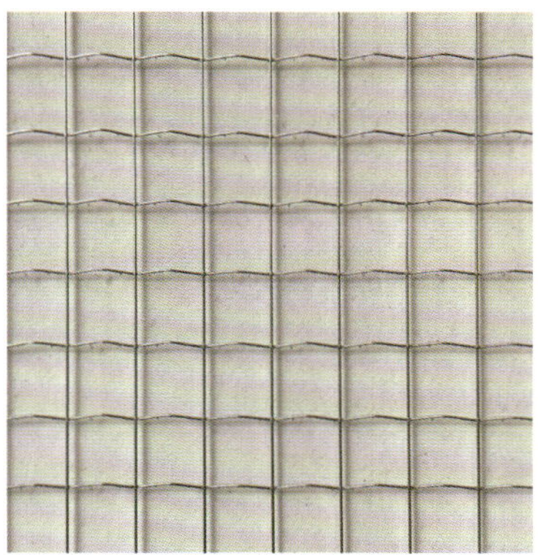
Wired glass

Bordiglio and Pentelicon stripe marble floor

Pair of Mallet Stevens armchairs covered in Kirkby Design / Bauhaus 1930s daybed with Bisson Bruneel / Art Déco modernist table / Bookcase clad in Sottsass veneer • **PHOTO 8** / Custom-designed JLD meeting table / Set of six vintage grey leather armchairs by Adnet / Bronze cup 200 BC / Bronze-era oil lamp-style candlestick / Porcelain decorative objects by Charlotte Feret / 1950s black wooden Italian sideboard • **PHOTO 9 & 10** / Pair of vintage girandoles with crystal *pampilles* / Plaster Diane de Poitiers bust / Pair of armchairs by Johannes Andersen in Boussac / Lacquered sideboard by Guy Lefevre for Maison Jansen / Set of four 1950s ball wall lamps / Mirror by Collection Pierre • **PHOTO 11** / Custom-designed JLD steel doors with wired glass elements and brass plate • **PHOTO 12** / Set of fourteen chairs by Marcel Breuer / Wall lights by Pouenat / Palm veneer center table by R&Y Augousti • **PHOTO 13** / Custom-designed JLD desk / Vintage 1950s table lamp / Custom-designed JLD mirror / Marble Apollon bust on a marble column • **PHOTO 14** / Wooden sideboard by Ordo / Marble urn / Set of four custom-designed JLD wall lamps / Small abstract painting by Flore Civazn Giudicelli / Abstract painting by G. Courlin • **PHOTO 16** / Pair of Louis XVI wall lights / Nineteenth-century Italian mirror • **PHOTO 17** / Porcelain tea set by Kazimir Malevich / Art Déco silver tea set / Eighteenth-century porcelain coffee set by Porcelaine de Limoges / Porcelain coffee set by Marie Daâge • **PHOTO 18** / 1980s modernist painting / Drawing table and chair that belonged to Charles de Sévigné / Set of four wall lights by Arlus • **PHOTO 21** / Table lamp by Arlus / Mirror custom designed by JLD for Pouenat / Plaster bust of Corneille •

LOS ANGELES
WEST HOLLYWOOD

Tucked away in the Sunset Hills just behind the famed Chateau Marmont hotel, the "Alice in Wonderland" house, as it's referred to in the neighborhood, is a lasting tribute to the glamorous Hollywood era of the 1930s and '40s. The quality and opulence that defined the essence of the period steered the principles of the house's design.

Anchored to a sprawling garden, the house becomes one element of a larger composition in which the outdoor and indoor areas are intertwined, making both spaces feel large and unobstructed. Together, they create a timeless space mixing past and present, weaving a seamless narrative of an authentic bygone Hollywood.

How do you feel about Los Angeles?

When I first arrived in Los Angeles, I was not looking for a Richard Neutra experience; in fact, I always felt the urge of the Old World. I love this city because there's so much eclecticism and everyone is on their own trip, which is what makes it fabulous!

This house was built in the 1930s with an interesting neo-Spanish structure. It made me think of Coco Chanel's La Pausa, a neo-medieval Spanish villa that she constructed in Roquebrun-Cap-Martin with ebony-stained oak flooring. I decided to have an all black-and-white color palette and instead of using darker Mediterranean furniture to suit the style of the space, I used light wood and straw marquetry to contrast and lighten up the space and bring sunny highlights to the interior.

Hollywood's glowing and luminescent light is an important element that you intensified.

The windows of the house aren't very big by today's standards, but there's incredible light that comes in naturally. In order to emphasize it, I placed the fishtail palms in front of the windows. Partially blocking the light gives you the impression of something being much brighter than it actually is.

I love the view at night when you see the whole town glittering and reflecting in the Tudor-style leaded-glass windows, which could be rather kitsch but work so well in this context.

Following pages: Photography by Hunter Kerhart

The first room is all about the ceiling...

I love the drama and the verticality of a cathedral ceiling. I never really know what to do with flat ceilings, so I always tend to dress them up with added architectural details; but when they are sloped, the elevated geometries are really interesting.

Each object has its predetermined place.

The placing of furniture in a room is like creating a three-dimensional set design. You have to take into consideration the overall view of the space and then give it depth and volume in order to accent specific areas. You have to decide which pieces will be in the foreground and which will disappear and complement in the background. I like to mix objects from different eras and even centuries to skew the notion of time.

The dialogue between the scale and the proportions of a room is always present for you.

You always need a monumental piece so that your eyes can read the true scale of the room and have a baseline for the right measurements. I placed the huge chandelier in the center and the enormous fishtail palms in front of the windows to emphasize the scale and the height of the room.

Today, the scale of furniture is made for much larger houses, so it was important to work around the original proportions of the rooms. I used a lot of French 1940s pieces from Jacques Adnet, whose modernist template combined functional designs with geometric simplicity, and André Arbus's purist, neoclassical-inspired armchairs. The banana-leaf carved light-oak Jansen game table would have looked tiny and inadequate somewhere else, but in this configuration is absolutely perfect.

Piet Hein Eek table

Gouged oak

Lesage embroidery inspired by Villa Kérylos

Custom-designed JLD cowhide rug

Coconut carpet

Moroccan woven fabric

PHOTO 2 / Spanish seventeenth-century chandelier with raffia custom shades by Anne Sokolsky / 1880s American bronze floor lamp / Early-American eighteenth-century armchair covered in natural raffia from Indonesia / 1940s Cubist anonymous painting / 1940s gueridon by André Groult / Eighteenth-century Swedish prince portrait / Mid-century ceramic lamp / Abstract stone sculpture by Anonymous • **PHOTO 3** / Mirror by Hervé Van Der Straeten / 1930s Serge Roche plaster wall lights / Alabaster globe light by Alain Ellouz / Oak sideboard by Jean-Michel Frank / Jean-Louis Deniot sofa for Baker upholstered in custom cotton fabric made in Tangiers • **PHOTO 4** / Armchair for Baker / Bronze urn by Hervé Van Der Straeten / Lamp by Tony Duquette / Custom-embroidery curtains based on the Villa Kérylos by Jean-François Lesage / Gold leaf capsule stool by Hervé Van Der Straeten / Coffee table in straw marquetery by Lison de Caunes • **PHOTO 5** / Custom-designed JLD white plaster chandelier / Sculpture by Hervé Van Der Straeten / Dining table by Piet Hein Herk / Bronze candlesticks by Garouste & Bonetti from David Gill / French 1940s oak chair by André Arbus covered in horsehair fabric by Le Crin / Curtain fabric by Harlequin / Hemp custom rug manufactured in India • **PHOTO 6** / Nineteenth-century Ethiopian leather shield, Arussi ethnic group / Mid-century straw and rope lamp purchased in Silver Lake, Los Angeles / Eighteenth-century terra-cotta vase from Morocco / French 1940s relief glazed terra-cotta abstract low / Set of eight oak chairs by Jacques Adnet upholstered in Brisson Bruneel / French 1940s oak console by Jean-Charles Moreux / Seventeenth-century colonial metal trunk • **PHOTO 7** / Giacometti-style coffee table with bronze base and stone top / Set of iron and wood chairs by Cleo Baldon / Set of vintage cushions from Morocco. • **PHOTO 8** / 1970s bronze wall lights by Curtis Jere / Nineteenth-century oak mirror / Natural-fiber wallpaper by Phillip Jeffries / 1940s stone obelisk, bronze bust and terra-cotta vase / Seventeenth-century African swords from Congo, formally Zaïre / Nineteenth-century African Sinufo tribe stool / Sofa by JLD for Baker upholstered in Nobilis / Bronze coffee table by Philip and Kelvin Laverne / 1940s ram-horn candlestick holders • **PHOTO 9** / T.H. Robsjohn-Gibbings-style daybed upholstered in vintage

African-inspired fabric "Makeba" by GSD

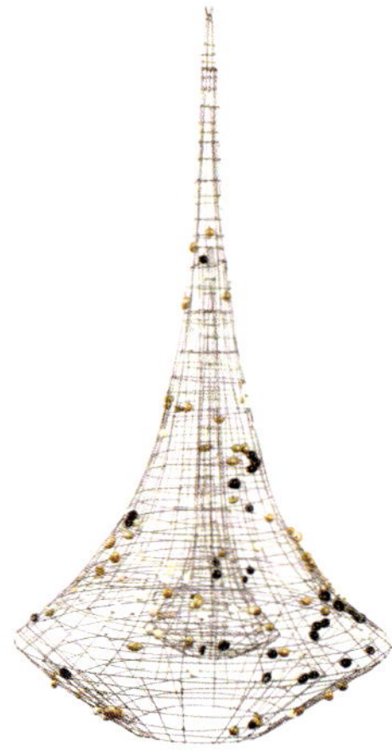

Custom-designed chandelier by Marie Christophe

Raffia-weave wallpaper by Phillip Jeffries

Bone

Rafia

Straw marquetry

Oxidized brass

fabric / Cushion in Holland & Sherry / Custom-designed JLD bronze and parchment bookcase • **PHOTO 10** / Roman-style terra-cotta fragment low relief / Mid-century ceramic lamp / Mid-century stained wood geometric table base / T.H. Robsjohn Gibbings-style chair upholstered in natural raffia / Area rug by Williams-Sonoma Home / 1940s plaster urn with floral design on mantel • **PHOTO 11** / 1940s French chandelier / 1940s French gold-leaf wall lights / Bone marquetery mirror by Karl Springer / Custom-designed JLD vanity front with brass acid front and bone leather knobs with chiseled limestone countertop • **PHOTO 12** / Custom-made chandelier with ceramic beads by Marie Christophe / Wood and tweed curtains / Vintage mirror / Wall reading lamp by JLD for Pouenat / Ethnic pillows from Morocco and vintage bolster from Togo, Africa / Mid-century bronze lamp • **PHOTO 13** / Chandelier by Tony Duquette / Nineteenth-century Etruscan-style bronze colonial bed / Mid-century lamp / French Art Déco gueridon / Hemp circular rug / Decorative cushions in Jim Thomson fabric and Kelly Wearstler cashmere bed cover • **PHOTO 14** / Slate mosaic mirror, rock crystal and pyrites by Béatrice Serre / Custom-designed JLD wall lights / Vintage eighteenth-century sink found in Istanbul / Cabinetry designed by JLD with bone knobs and antique stone top • **PHOTO 15** / 1970s window salon chairs by Sido and François Thévenin / Seventeenth-century rock crystal candlestick mounted as lamp / Collection of crystal balls from the Coco Chanel suite at the Ritz / Maison Jansen 1940s banana leaf game table • **PHOTO 16** / Custom-designed JLD convex mirror / Lanterns from Marrakesh / Vintage pillows from Tangier / Sunbrella outdoor fabric, sand color / African cave plate / Ten-foot-long casted cement firepit with molded side planks custom designed by Scott Shrader with volcanic stone centerpiece • **PHOTO 17** / Custom-designed stone bar by JLD / Frederick Weinberg stool / Vintage ten-foot-long dining table with a bronze base and limestone top / Rattan chairs from Buttercup • **PHOTO 19** / Wall light by Scott Shrader / Vintage 1900s convex mirror from Bruno Le Yaouanc Paris / Outdoor fireplace design by JLD, clad in flagstone matching terrace flooring / Large windmill stone used as an eight-foot-long coffee table / Set of African stools •

NEW YORK
UPPER EAST SIDE

For a prominent New England family, this Upper East Side townhouse could easily have become a Manhattan trophy house, but instead it was transformed into a true family home. The facade, which has protected landmark status, imparts a sense of permanence and tradition to what seems from the outside to be a classical residence. The back of the house was demolished and entirely rebuilt to bring in a downtown industrial vocabulary conveying a fresh air of modernity.

You started by introducing a downtown narrative to an uptown address.

By blending the archetypes of an emblematic townhouse with a neo-industrial look, I was able to treat the space as a giant loft, allowing me to maximize the amount of light, but also to close off areas with respect to specific functions. I was able to bring the best of both worlds: uptown conventions and downtown freedom.

How was a balanced distribution of living areas created?

This project was a very joyful process in finding the perfect layout to accommodate a recomposed family. What's fantastic about the plan is that it preserves everyone's privacy, while maximizing everyone's comfort. The two older kids have their suite on the ground floor with a great hangout family room area, a fantastic spot to invite their friends. On the second floor, you have the reception rooms and a huge kitchen in the back as well as the primary bedroom floor. On the top floor, you have the quarters for the younger kids.

Photography by Jonny Valiant

You look to use both form and function.

It's always a nice equation. In the kitchen, I introduced *voutins*, small ceiling arches typically found in industrial buildings at the end of the nineteenth century, not only to act as light reflectors but also to hide the led-strip electric lighting system. The entire kitchen ceiling is invisibly lit. The use of industrial elements helps the room to feel architectural and low-key while correcting and implementing a natural flow in the space.

The living room has a formal vocabulary, but it's very comfortable.

I didn't have the footprint to make it a really grand living room but it opens onto the hall, which becomes a direct extension and breaks the visual limit between both spaces. The furniture on the

landing had to fit the double function of defining the look and feel of a proper landing at the foot of a sweeping staircase and, at the same time, it needed to feel like an annex of the living room.

I had really good height in this room, and designing vertical paneling allowed me to stretch the elevation even more. I generally like to do double seating, toward the fireplace or directly opposite, allowing the sitters to enjoy the whole perspective. In this instance, that solution wasn't going to

work because we didn't have the space. We went with a circular seating plan to give a more dynamic and expansive feeling. It also allows people to travel in their own sitting room. The rug I designed amplifies the idea of a splash with paint drips projecting out to suggest movement. All of these elements allowed me to create a grand effect out of a normal-size room.

And the dining room then takes you in a very different direction.

Generally, dining rooms in France or Europe command the most festive and opulent decors, where richness is to be displayed. There's a crescendo in the room sequencing that culminates in the dining room. I vaulted the ceilings, opened the iron windows, and made all the doors to match.

When they are closed, the doors are outfitted in mirror and black iron bringing symmetry and balance to the room. You have the impression you're surrounded by openings but there's only a single window, which is wedged in the corner. All the others are mere reflections.

I commissioned Florence Girette to paint a fabulous summer night sky with gold dust outlines. The resulting abstract wall treatment is open to interpretation, as everyone has their own take, but the reason the decor works well is because the base is very dark and the abstract pattern is done by layering the paint. Setting a festive ambiance, the light from the two chandeliers by Hervé Van Der Straeten reproduces shimmering shadows throughout the room.

Fluted-plaster walls

Custom-designed JLD rug by Diurne

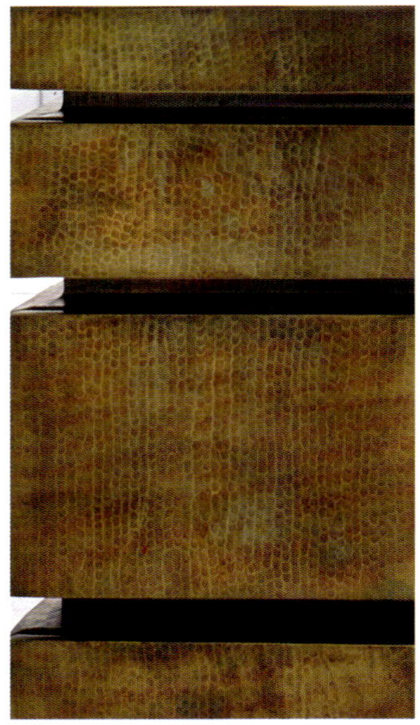
Custom-designed JLD dresser in hammered brass

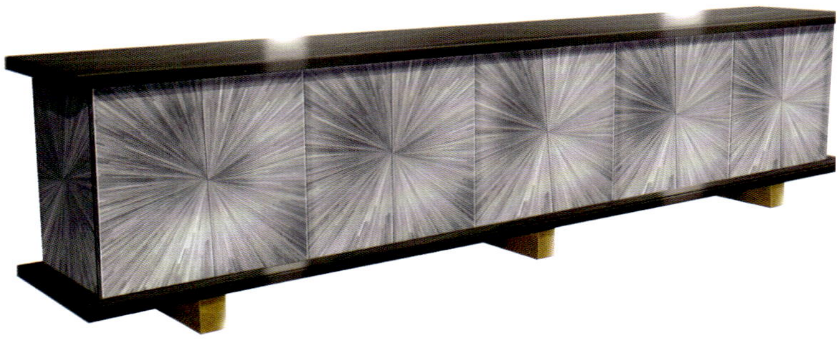
Custom-designed JLD sideboard

Straw marquetry

PHOTO 1 / Antique Louis XV console table from France / Pair of 1950s Italian armchairs / Set of Kelly Wearstler sconces • **PHOTO 2** / Custom-designed Jean-Louis Deniot lacquered wood bench in Rubelli fabric / Pair of wall lights "Hyperbole" by Hervé Van Der Straeten • **PHOTO 3** / Alabaster globe light by Alain Ellouz / Black marquina Louis XIV-style fireplace from Paris / Pair of custom-designed JLD andirons / Pair of 1940s wall lights by André Arbus • **PHOTO 4** / Wallpaper by Omexco / Custom-designed JLD rug by Solstys / Chandelier by Hervé Van Der Straeten / Custom-designed JLD sofas upholstered in Boussac with Houlès piping / Pair of 1950s floor lamps by Diderot Edition / Coffee table by Michael Mangematin / Tripod brass and glass gueridon by Poggi / Custom-designed JLD pedestal in hammered brass / Brass candlesticks by JHQ Dansk design / Panting by Alfredo Ulloa / Glass centerpiece by Alexa Lixfeld • **PHOTO 5** / Decorative mural by Florence Girette / Custom-designed JLD area rug by Solstys / Pair of chandeliers "Lustre à Facettes" by Hervé Van Der Straeten / Custom-designed JLD dining table / Set of Empire candlesticks / Dining chairs "Comédie Ovale" by Counot Blandin covered in Osborne & Little / Antique Louis XVI-style marble fireplace

Custom-designed JLD rug by Diurne

Mural by Florence Girette

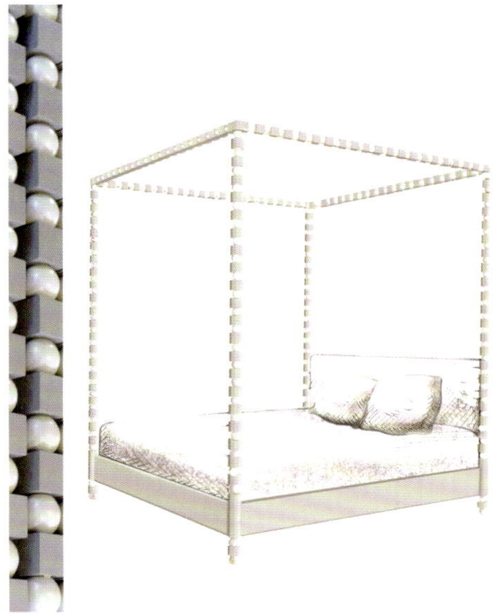

Custom-designed JLD four-poster bed

Grey "Rainbow" wallpaper by Oxmeco

"Storm" fabric by Boussac

from Paris / Mirror "Nebuleuse" by Hervé Van Der Straeten • **PHOTO 6** / Custom-designed JLD sideboard in black-lacquered wood and straw marquetry / Ceramic lamp by James Mont • **PHOTO 8** / Table by Knoll / Set of chairs by Kai Kristiansen upholstered in Kvadrat / 1950s gilt bronze candlesticks / Louis XV-style antique rock-crystal chandelier / Barstools by Midj / Sculpture by Barbro Åberg • **PHOTO 9** / Pair of curtains in Lelièvre and Création Baumann / Custom-designed JLD lacquered wood bed canopy and headboard covered in Brochier / Pair of nightstands by T.H. Robsjohn-Gibbings / Pair of brutalist lamps by Harry Balmer, lampshades by Anne Sokolsky in Petra Tlapova painted silk • **PHOTO 10** / 1970s lantern attributed to Angelo Brotto / Pair of long 1970s Murano glass wall lights / Lapiz Lazuli sculpture from Creel and Gow • **PHOTOS 11 & 12** / Wall-to-wall carpet by Stark Carpet / Custom JLD wallpaper by Porter Teleo / Mirror "Fizzy" by Hervé Van Der Straeten / 1960s textured glass bubble ceiling light / Custom-designed JLD central island in hammered brass finish / Custom-designed JLD rock-crystal brass and iron andirons / Blue glass sculpture by Dale Chihuly from Maison Gérard •

NEW YORK
CHELSEA

Situated in the heart of Chelsea's gallery district, in architect Annabelle Selldorf's first large-scale building, this duplex penthouse with panoramic views of the Hudson River brings together the spectacular display of uninterrupted sky, the shimmering waterway and the Manhattan urban cityscape. There is the added amenity of an impressive apartment-level parking elevator that deposits residents and their cars directly at their doorstep.

With such an impressive space, what was your inspiration?

It's all based on the reflections off the water. When I first walked into the living room, it was like being in a floating basketball court because it's an immense space, with nearly 23-foot ceilings. A double height terrace continues outside and prolongs the weightlessness of the interior, dazzling with impressive views of Lower Manhattan. The clouds are literally hovering at your height and the river reflections echo inside the space. To intensify the effect, the apartment is sparsely furnished in keeping with the overall ethereal ambiance.

It is for this interior that you commissioned an exceptional set of the curtains.

It was important to provide a second layer of interest in this room. Even if you have spectacular views, when it's pitch-black outside looking onto the river, the fully glazed giant windows limit the options of what you can do. At the same time, I wanted to keep the feel of an artist's studio or at least a bare interior like the one at the Maison de Verre, Pierre Chareau's iconic 1920s house in Paris. I commissioned a set of eight exceptional 23-foot-high curtains embroidered with abstract patterns simulating the reflection of a water landscape for when it's pitch black outside on the river. Each panel in the series is unique and accentuates the diversity and fluidity of the effect.

Photography by Stephan Julliard

You collaborated with famed French embroiderer Jean-François Lesage. What did you discuss?

Initially, I was worried that the embroidered curtains would be too rich and imposing. The clients were coming from a sprawling Fifth Avenue home, and I wanted them to be in a more modern space.

It was important for the curtain elements to be elaborate but not ostentatious. As a base, I chose a thick Pierre Frey linen, with a dégradé (gradient) color of beige, pearl, and deep blue.

Treating the gradation vertically emphasized the impressive height of the space. The embroidery in round and square cannetilles in four bronze tones with organza, and satin applications runs almost the full height of the curtains. It was hammered to give an uneven sheen so as to better evoke the water reflection. To keep the airy effect, the curtain rods are invisible, imbedded directly in the ceiling plaster.

The living room has a very different personality at night.

I placed delicate, almost invisible, cocoon-shaped chandeliers that look like golden spider webs in daylight. At night, they light up the space and cast astonishing shadows on the ceiling, creating a lyrical effect with the passing clouds. The méridienne (short sofa) has an open back to let the light pass through unobstructed. The carpet pattern was based on a striking marble slab that was redefined with new colorations to mimic the water element. Instead of the traditional black lacquer, the vintage Steinway piano was restored in a blue matte finish keeping with the lightness of the room.

In the back of the apartment, you transformed the second terrace to form a double-height family room.

I arrived on the project early enough that we were able to make the modification. I don't mind if a space has a small footprint, but what I really care about is the ceiling height. And I went back to the French enfilade system where there's a crescendo in the decor throughout the journey of the walk-through. Enclosing the terrace was like the cherry on the cake, allowing me to make a family

MISSION TO PARIS

DOSSIER
THE SECRET HISTORY OF ARMAND HAMMER
EDWARD JAY EPSTEIN
AMERICAN SOLDIER
THE HIDDEN OASIS

THE HIDDEN OASIS
PAUL SUSSMAN

room that can also serve as a dining room. At the switch of a button, the cocktail table rises to dining level.

I designed the plated-copper ribbon chandelier lined with antique brass to unify the room's dual personalities. As a family room, it brings a playful element to the space and when lit for dinner it shimmers and amplifies the stunning downtown views, which become the main spectacle.

Pierre Frey fabric

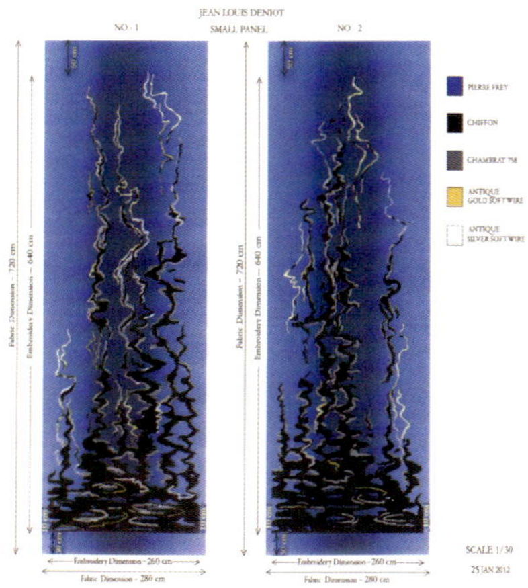

Back-painted glass by Florence Girette

Custom-designed Lesage embroidery

Chandelier by Ombre Portée

PHOTO 1 / "Pebble Marble" coffee table by Nada Debs / Sofa by Janus et Cie / Blue cushions in Dominique Picquier / Plastic rug manufactured in Senegal • **PHOTO 2** / Vintage Steinway custom lacquered in a matte finish / Silk rug by Tai Ping / 1950s Stilnovo opaline floor lamp / Pouf by Ochre upholstered in two tones of suede / Vintage Gio Ponti armchair with is original ivory leather and suede / Side table in bronze and shagreen by R&Y Augousti • **PHOTO 3** / Custom-designed Jean-Louis Deniot bench upholstered in "Bouleaux" by Créations Métaphores / Set of cushions covered in linen "Leo" by Pierre Frey / Bronze and back-painted glass coffee table by JLD for Jean de Merry / Serpentine sofa by Vladimir Kagan upholstered in "Douala" by Armani Casa / Sculpture *Pluto* in reinforced gypsum and fiberglass (behind the sofa) by Robert Taplin / Diptych painting *Die Ungeborenen Neimandrose* (above the stairs) by Anselm Kiefer / Custom-designed JLD back-painted glass fireplace / Artwork *Triptych* (above the fireplace) by Mauro Perucchetti / Lacquer and bronze bar (underneath the stairs) by Hervé Van Der Straeten • **PHOTO 4** / 1950s biscuit lamp, custom metallic shade by Anne Sokolsky / Side table "Abyssus" by McCollin Bryan / Vintage sofa by Edward Wormley upholstered in three different tones of a distressed velvet "Bosfora" by Brochier / Set of cushions covered in cotton "Baxan" by Jim Thompson, and "Deluxe" by Zimmer+Rohde / Curtains are made in linen "Kalahari" by Pierre Frey embroidered by Jean-François Lesage to mimic water reflection • **PHOTO 5** / Brass ceiling lights by Ombre Portée / Bronze coffee table "Goutte d'Eau" by Ado Challe • **PHOTO 6** / Chrome and Macassar

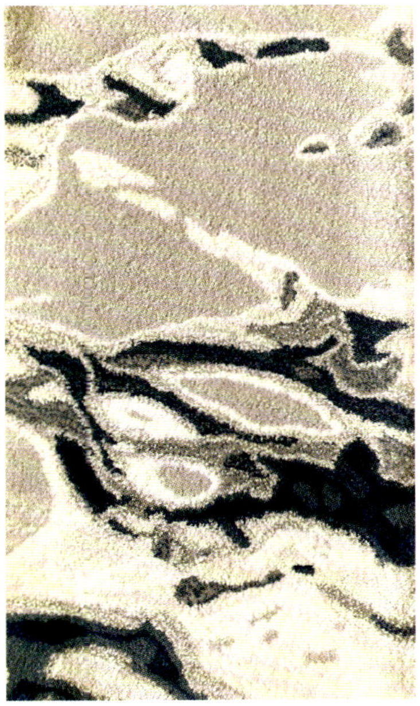
Rug by Tai Ping

"Bouleau" by Créations Métaphores

Custom-designed bar by Hervé Van Der Straeten

Bone marquetry

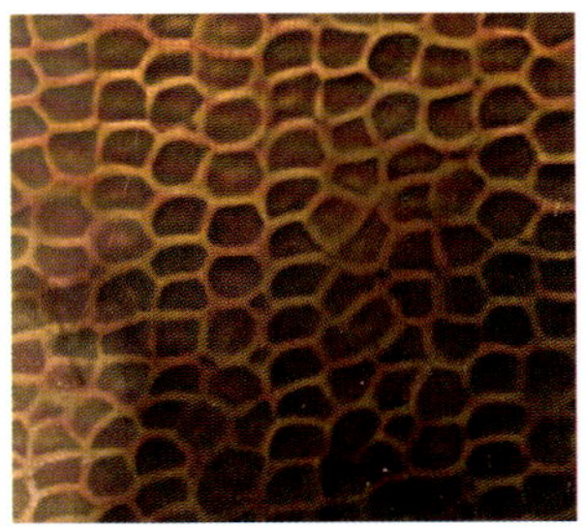
Distressed hammered brass

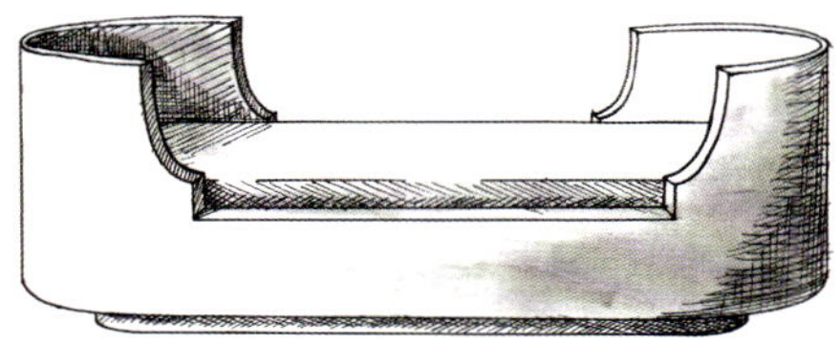
Custom-designed JLD daybed

ebony "Archipelago" table designed by Guy de Rougemont / Set of swivel chairs by Le Corbusier and Pierre Jeanneret / Wallpaper "Metallic Paper Weaves" by Phillip Jeffries / Painting from Michal Rovner's *Border* series / Custom-designed JLD banquette covered in Dedar embroidered by Jean-François Lesage with stainless-steel and silk thread • **PHOTO 7** / Custom-designed JLD island made in marquetry of polished stainless steel, brushed stainless steel, ash-stained teak and ebony-stained teak, top and sides in brushed black granite / Custom-designed JLD pendant lights with glass globes by John Pomp • **PHOTO 8** / Custom copper and brass ribbon chandelier by Ombre Portée / Custom-designed JLD electric bone-topped table / Custom designed JLD armchairs upholstered in "Quintin" by Hodsoll McKenzie / Curtains in linen "Span" by Christopher Farr • **PHOTO 9** / Custom-designed JLD wall-to-wall carpet by Tai Ping / Custom-designed JLD forged-iron bookshelves in brushed and lacquered oak • **PHOTO 10** / Walls in "Branchage" by Dominique Picquier / Custom-designed JLD headboard covered in two tones of "Brianza" velvet by Sanderson / Ceramic bedside lamp by Véronique Rivemale / Custom-designed JLD hammered-bronze nightstand / Cushions in "Cobbles" from Pasaya • **PHOTO 12** / Bath surround made in Vals Stone - Switzerland / Bathtub by Jacob Delafon / Tap and shower fixture, "Henry" collection from Waterworks / Custom-designed JLD dark-bronze frames wall lights

MIAMI
SOUTH BEACH

The sky is really the only limit for this striking penthouse floating above the beach in Miami. The perfect backdrop to Miami's Art Deco scene, it brings together a European sophistication with the oceanside sex appeal of the South Beach scene. For the structural elements, Herzog & de Meuron's astonishing concrete car park in Miami serves as a key inspiration. The influences of Constantin Brancusi's atelier in Paris balance the rawness of the space by producing generous volumes and spectacular light.

An ode to the artist studio, you introduced a more brutalist aesthetic to this apartment.

It was initially decorated as an antique Spanish castle with travertine columns, orange patina, forged-iron wall lights and shiny marble. The first thing I did was to demolish it completely. When the cement started to appear underneath, it had a very mineral quality to it and I decided to treat it like a local coral stone. It instantly made the apartment feel so much more legitimate and authentic instead of hiding behind painted cardboard walls.

In order to keep the structure completely exposed, we diverted all the wiring and technical elements into one single section which permitted the rest of the space to stay pure and bare. I've always been fascinated by the light and volume of artist studios. It seemed so appropriate to work on this theme here where the biggest art fair in the world, Art Basel Miami, is held every year.

Photography by Stephan Julliard

You love high ceilings. And here, you're on the 26th floor flying above South Beach.

We were lucky because this building was developed before the height regulation in the 1980s. What I love most about the view is the birds fly at your eye level and so do the airplanes. This apartment is a true nest. The irony is that the exposed concrete doesn't give the impression of heaviness or bulk. Quite the contrary, it is airy and gives a feeling of lightness, like clouds in a way.

The transition between indoors and out is seamless...

Yes, to achieve that effect the rug was designed for outdoor use so it can sit inside or out and it's split so that the sliding glass doors can close. Most of the fabrics are actually for outdoors in case you leave the window open or simply want to drag furniture outside. Neither the terrace nor the living room are particularly large in size. By having the carpet roll out in both spaces, and having the same ceiling height between the indoor and the outdoors, it gives the impression that the room is double the size because the dividing windows disappear visually, creating a continuous space.

The furniture that you used is quite generous in size.

Most of the pieces are vintage and were chosen for their sense of style and comfort. They also needed to be on a large scale to balance the room's exceptional height. The sofa is giant, the concrete head on a pedestal is massive and, for a sense of scale, the 1920s terrazzo nose fragment is more than two feet tall. The armchairs are Jindrich Halabala from the 1930s and introduce a link with the Art Deco South Beach buildings. On the terrace, I wanted to give a sense of movement, so I chose a rocking chair in rattan. All of the seating has in common a posture of ease. In a New York City apartment, you could put a pair of armchairs in the main salon that are very beautiful but not the most comfortable. Here, you want to be relaxed in a bathing suit and low-key ambiance.

How did you treat lighting through the rooms?

For the entrance and corridor, I created a long wall of brass panels to capture and intensify the light and warmth of the sun. When you enter a space on the 26th floor in Miami, you expect a shot of sunshine, not a dark hall. The panels not only act like mirrors but also hide all the doors to give a more seamless visual result. In the kitchen, the cabinet reflections you see are actually lasered abstract patterns printed on stainless steel to give the impression that the kitchen is liquid.

The master bedroom didn't benefit from the same ceiling height as the other spaces, and I wanted to open it up. Since the room is square, I had the idea of placing a decorative painted canvas with a storm-like water aureole effect to create height and to give the ceiling depth and movement.

Casted concrete wall finish

Custom-designed JLD breakfast table

White-painted terra-cotta bricks

Terrazzo floor

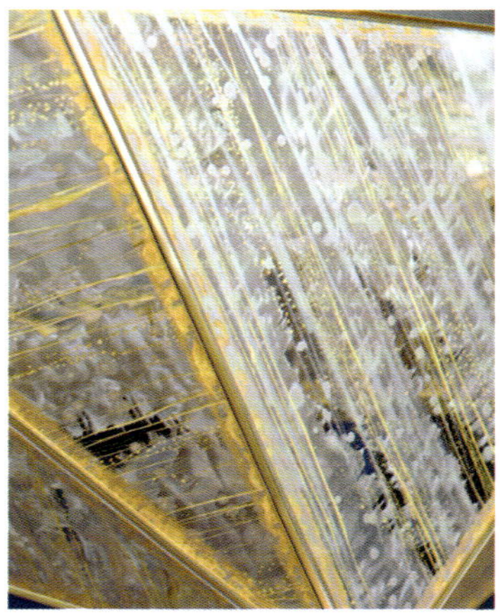
Back-painted glass

Polished-brass mirror

PHOTO 1 / Custom-designed Jean-Louis Deniot outdoor quality carpet by Diurne / 1920s French Villa Kerylos Greco Roman-design chandelier in bronze and alabaster • **PHOTOS 2 & 4** / Custom-designed JLD sofa for Baker covered in a cotton by Martyn Thompson Studio / Custom-designed JLD cement, plaster, bronze floor spots / Custom-designed JLD distressed-stone drums side table / Vintage coffee table / Custom-designed JLD bronze and glass hurricane candle holder / Custom-designed JLD table lamp in back-painted glass by Florence Girette and bronze trims by Schmidt Bronzier, Paris / Pair of 1930s chairs by Jindrich Halabala in JAB Anstoelz, Houlès piping • **PHOTO 3** / Vintage Ilmari Taplovaara rocking chair / 1960s rattan chair covered in outdoor Kravet / Marble side table from Paris flea market • **PHOTO 5** / Custom-designed JLD television cabinet with doors in blue straw marquetry and wood lacquer on XXL's ball base / Artwork by Jérôme Robbe

Ceiling painting by Florence Girette

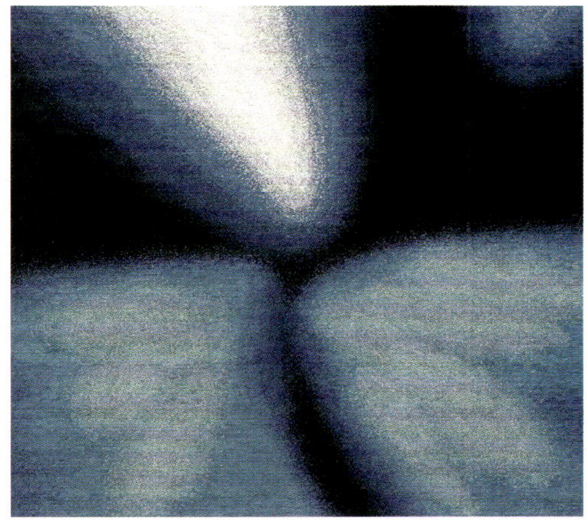

Custom-designed JLD rug by Diurne

Straw marquetry

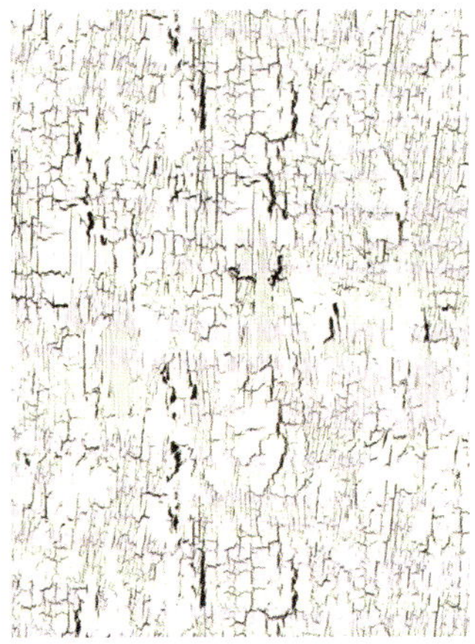

Crackled velvet by Romo

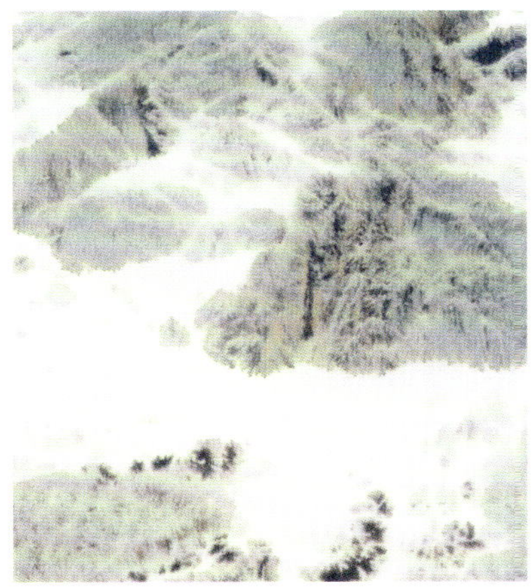

Cotton fabric by Martyn Thompson

/ French 1930s table lamp from Teo Leo, Paris • **PHOTO 6** / Custom-designed JLD breakfast table with brass legs and decorative lacquered balls and stone top / American mid-century armchairs in printed crackled velvet by Romo / Custom-designed JLD iridescent-glass ceiling light / Vintage blue-opaline Murano from the 1950s • **PHOTO 7** / Abstract pattern laser-printed on stainless cabinet front / Dornbracht and Franke sink fittings / Terrazzo flooring / Vintage 1950s gold-leaf oval mirror • **PHOTOS 8 & 9** / Polished-brass wall panels / Custom-designed JLD dark bronze ceiling lights • **PHOTO 10** / Custom-designed JLD floor lamp, black iron, lampshade by Anne Sokolsky / Large articulated wall light in polished brass by JLD for Pouenat / Ceiling painting canvas by Florence Girette / Bedcover in Romo, Houlès piping / Bed pillow in Lelièvre, Houlès piping • **PHOTO 11** / Wall lights by Jonathan Browning • Custom-designed JLD marble sink •

MIAMI
FLAMINGO DRIVE

This archetypal mid-century single-story house pays tribute to the quintessential Art Deco architect Morris Lapidus who defined the Miami modernist movement in the 1950s and '60s, exemplified by his iconic Fontainebleau Hotel nearby. The perfect backdrop to the Miami Beach lifestyle, this house plays on the visual narratives of those bygone eras and adds a layer referencing the 1980s hit television series *Miami Vice*. Its architectural innovations bring the spaciousness of a warehouse industrial space into a private home environment.

There is a theatricality to this home with a 1950s allure.

The open space is really suited to that narrative. It creates a cinematographic opportunity to direct the flow. From the entrance, you see the sitting room and the bar in the back inviting you to grab a drink. You continue to the second lounge area from where the dining table can be seen. At this point, your glass may be empty and you walk toward the pool area and get a refill at the outside bar before heading to dinner. The design proposes different narratives of what you can do when you arrive. The functionality indicates how to actually behave. We always say that something is sexy because it's very suggestive and here, the design defines the undeniable sex appeal of this house.

You often work with open space concepts that are adjustable but with this project it was particularly fluid.

French layouts always include doors or archways to introduce a visual and structural rhythm. In this instance, the outlined areas are much less definite, and it's one of the few times they are not defined by any vertical elements. The limited number of steps between zones suffices to visually separate planes and make the junctions even if there is limited wall space.

Photography by Stephan Julliard

There are few walls for hanging art.

Art is part of an environment but it's not the environment itself. In my work, I always include perspectives with simple or double doors, large windows, and paneling, which leave minimum amount of wall space for art. There are many things that I can control in a project: the architecture, interior design, circulation, lighting, color palette. The one thing I cannot control is the client's personal art collection. In order to do it justice, I like to isolate the art near a set of doors or panels flanking the piece so that it's not about matching the artwork with the drapes.

What guided your choices for the placement of the furniture?

In creating the layout, I give people options to be front and center stage, or to be more on the periphery. If you want to feel like the center of attraction, you have a front row seat in every room; but if you feel you want to catch up with a good friend and sit in a more relaxed corner, you also have that option. The multiple configurations provide different possibilities, and it's up to the guests to decide what experience they want. I love that play on momentum.

Because the spaces are large, you need them to be convenient and functional. You can easily end up with too many components and create a physical and visual traffic jam. You have to limit the juxtapositions of too many visuals within the same frame.

For this project, your choice of flooring is a very tactile experience.

The relation of the indoor-outdoors was super important. To emphasize the fact that there's no transition between interior and exterior, the flooring throughout is identical terrazzo, poured and casted on-site with the added plus that walking barefoot on this type of flooring is just fabulous. I love the idea that you have no transition of surface under your feet. Throughout the property, you walk on the same identical floor.

What informed the fabric designs and schemes?

The Miami sun is so strong and intense, it was difficult to choose. Tie-dye comes from a completely different part of the world, and it didn't make sense. I needed strong eye-catching patterns and decided to use wax fabric. By choosing these African print fabrics, I get the graphics, the colors, and the sunshine. They give the impression of belonging to the Miami vibe—but because of their striking patterns and how they react to the dominant light.

Is there one magical element?

It's a combination... You light a few candles. Put the music on. And you are ready to go. It's like sexy time on the switch.

PALACIO DE LAS GARZAS
INDIA

Custom rug by Solstys

Raku ceramic

Custom rug by Solstys

"Collage Marine" fabric by Robert Normand

Custom-designed JLD door handle and plate

Brushed and flamed granite

PHOTO 1 / Terrazzo flooring / Custom-designed JLD bar and outdoor furniture • **PHOTO 2** / Pedestal "Heliodor" by Jean-Louis Deniot for Baker / Sculpture by Angel Ortiz / "Topaz" Mirror by JLD for Baker • **PHOTO 3** / Custom-designed JLD area rug by Solstys / Vintage pair of armchairs in Karin Sajo / Black side table "Heliodor Accent" by JLD for Baker / Three custom-designed JLD coffee tables with fossilized wood top, grey stain oak top, and distressed-bronze top • **PHOTO 4** / Coffee table "Citrine" by JLD for Baker / Pair of armchairs by JLD for Baker in Kvadrat and Boubou / Side table "Sphalerit" by JLD for Baker / Pair of mid-century floor lamps • **PHOTO 5** / Custom-designed JLD raku ceramic ceiling lights / Wing-shape sofa in Pierre Frey / Set of cushions, Cleo and Pierre Frey / Set of four vintage bar stools in Robert Normand / Table lamp "Obsidian" by JLD for Baker / Mirror "Tourmaline" by JLD for Baker • **PHOTO 6** / Custom-designed JLD sectional sofa covered in Rogers & Goffigon / Set of cushions in Rubelli, Edmond Petit, and African wax fabric, Houlès piping • **PHOTO 7** / Chandelier "Lolite" by JLD for Baker / Custom-designed JLD dining table / Custom-designed JLD pair of plexiglass benches / Pair of dining chairs "Iron Eve" by JLD for Baker upholstered in African wax fabric / Burl

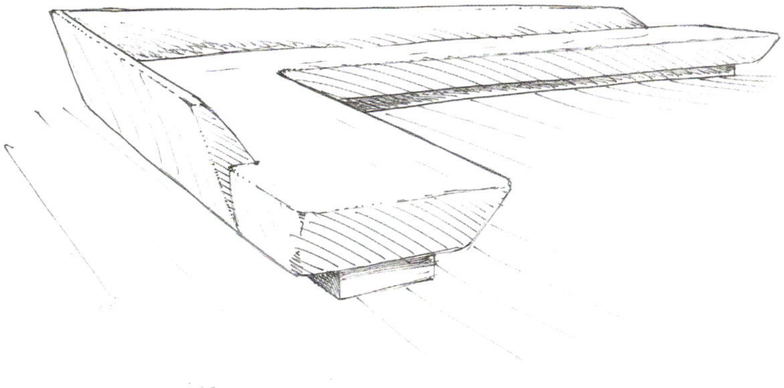

Custom-designed JLD sofa

Custom rug manufactured by Solstys

Blue matte lacquered cabinet by Hervé Van Der Straten

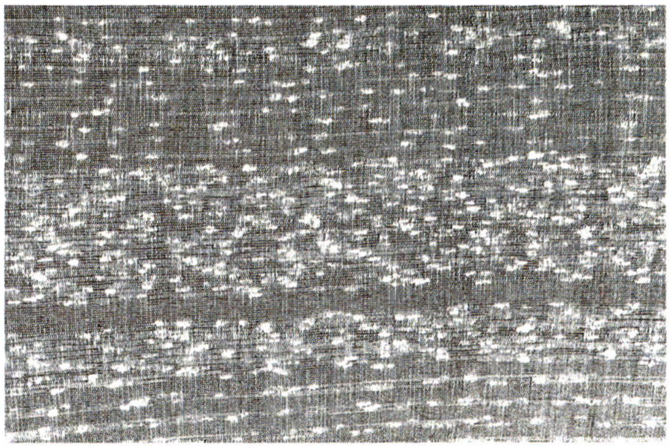

Custom woven Moroccan fabric

wood 1950s sideboard / Art by Enrique Riveron and Maria Gonzales • **PHOTO 8** / Ceiling light by Curtis Jeer / Mirror "Chrysoprase" by JLD for Baker / Painting by Andre Brandao from Iconic Design Gallery • **PHOTO 9** / Custom-designed JLD rug by Solstys / Sofa "Almandi" by JLD for Baker in custom grey bouclette, cushions in African wax fabric / Pair of vintage 1950s floor lamps / Vintage American office chair / 1960s Californian desk / Pair of curtains in "camouflage" Dominique Kieffer by Rubelli / Vintage 1950s French chandelier / Painting by Isabelle Gougenheim / Mid-century side table • **PHOTOS 10 & 14** / Custom-designed JLD area rug by Solstys / Headboard covered in Rubelli, Houlès piping / Custom-embroidered pillows / Mirror "Amétrine" by JLD for Baker / Pair of bedside tables by Gio Ponti / Custom-designed JLD, bench, brass structure, upholstered in ivory bouclette / Pair of table lamps "Iron Eye" by JLD for Baker / Blue sculpture cabinet by Hervé Van Der Straeten / Alabaster globe by Alain Ellouz • **PHOTO 11** / Set of ceramic art pieces by Stephanie Bergman • **PHOTO 13** / Vintage bean shape sofa in Boussac / Custom-designed JLD floor lamp / African wooden stool •

CALI
COLOMBIA

A passionate ambassador not only for her native Colombia but also for the distinctive cultural heritage of her people, Nancy Gonzalez, the world-renowned accessories designer, supports a vision of personal growth, tolerance, and the pursuit of excellence. The aesthetic pillars of her brand—purity, balance and composition--served as the guiding principles for the transformation of her two-story residence. In the city of Cali, her homeland, rich landscapes and luscious gardens filled with exuberant vegetation are ever present. Achieving the perfect balance between function and creativity, this home amplifies her core values without altering their essence.

The archetypical South American woman, Nancy Gonzalez exudes qualities of inner strength, audacious conviction, and true elegance.

She's extremely refined and always prefers less, but excellent. Santiago, her son, reached out to me when she acquired the flat. Her home really reflects her sense of precision. She's exceptionally detailed in her choices, but is always open and appreciates new and different points of view. Her elegance comes with a timelessness and a certain way of living in which integrity and values are ever present. For Nancy, the highest form of luxury is to have options, and it was important in the overall design to stay true to her principles.

At the time, this was one of the most contemporary spaces you had ever worked on.

Yes. Normally, I feel comfortable with open plans because I am able to use floor finishes or door openings as transitions. In this case, I had to keep the loft ambiance while defining specific functions tc particular areas. One solution I found was to work on various ceiling treatments to visually outline the space in each room. In the dining area it's a square with a cove, while the living room has a big oval ceiling. The French limestone flooring is identical inside and out, creating a feeling of seamless continuity when the doors are open to reveal the extravagant collection of wild orchids that decorate the garden trees.

Photography by Anita Calero

The living room is both graceful and surprising.

Elegance comes with the unexpected, even if it feels as if you couldn't imagine it in any other way. Actually, it's a very large living room. To give a sense of scale, the daybed in the center is a king size, on which you can lay or sit on either side. When you have a very large room, it's not about

multiplying the seating, because it can end up looking like a hotel lobby. It's about thoughtfully placing the seats so you can sit by yourself just as easily as you can sit in small groups.

Elegance can also come from a form of relaxed nonchalance, which gives a fluidity in the choice of objects. Her exacting curation of artistic works includes a grouping with a beautiful seventeenth-

century Madonna, a stunning gold woven textile piece by pioneering Columbian artist Olga de Amaral, a series of exceptional pre-Colombian necklaces, a Candida Höfer photograph, and the iconic Yves Klein blue and gold leaf table. Together they illustrate a true portrait of her personal style.

How did you use the transition from inside to out?

When the sliding windows open, you have giant fractions of the walls which literally disappear. The floor is continuous, and we used indoor-looking furniture outside. The outdoors becomes another sitting room. You have no transition in-between, and you're privy to sweeping views of the exceptional landscape.

It's all about the surface treatments...

There are textures literally everywhere. The dining chairs offer a striking example. Each chair is covered in ivory-colored matte crocodile with sand-toned horsehair-lined backs. A transparent horsehair slipcover protects and dresses up the precious materials. And the dining table is in straw marquetry. The juxtaposition of the translucent horsehair with the crocodile on the back of the French chairs is worthy of couture-level craftsmanship and excellence, which perfectly reflects the project's level of sophistication.

Horsehair by Le Crin

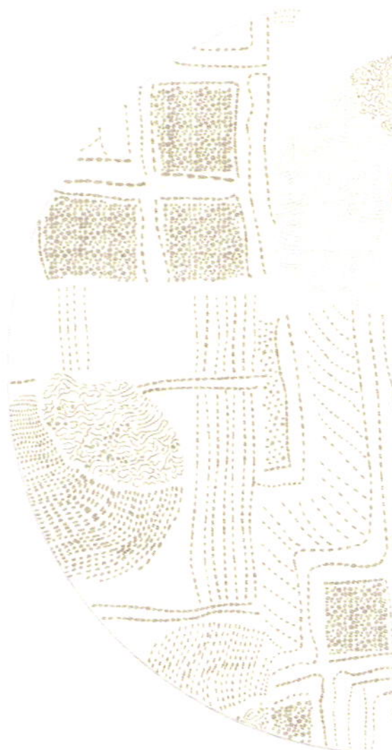

Custom-designed JLD rug by Diurne

Custom-designed JLD chair

White matte crocodile

Custom-designed JLD door handle

Silk velvet by Brunschwig

PHOTOS 1 & 2 / Pair of "Rita" armchairs by Jean-Louis Deniot for Collection Pierre upholstered with cotton velvet by Romo / Mid-century French brass and black opaline asymmetrical floor lamp with table tops / Large Empire daybed in grey patina and gilt accent in Romo linen / Custom-designed JLD rug by Diurne / Art piece of woven leather and gold leaf by Olga de Amaral / Curtains in Sahco • **PHOTO 3** / Floor lamp by Gaetano Scolari, Paris / Mid-century floor lamp with tray, lampshade by Anne Sokolsky / Pair of coffee tables (blue pigment, gold-leaf lucite and stainless steel) by Yves Klein / Large sofa by JLD for Collection Pierre in Métaphores cotton bouclette / Pair of bronze chairs by Lalanne / Art piece by Candida Höfer / Gold pre-Colombian jewelry • **PHOTO 5** / Patinated bronze chandelier "Palmes" by Hervé Van der Straeten / Set of dining chairs by JLD for Pierre Counot Blandin covered with white matte crocodile / Custom-designed JLD straw marquetry dining table / Custom-designed JLD rug by Diurne • **PHOTO 6** / Pair of gilt wrought-iron lounge chairs by Rodger Thibier in Brunschwig silk velvet / Vintage ceramic table lamp in the style of Georges

Wall textured plaster

Warm brown oak

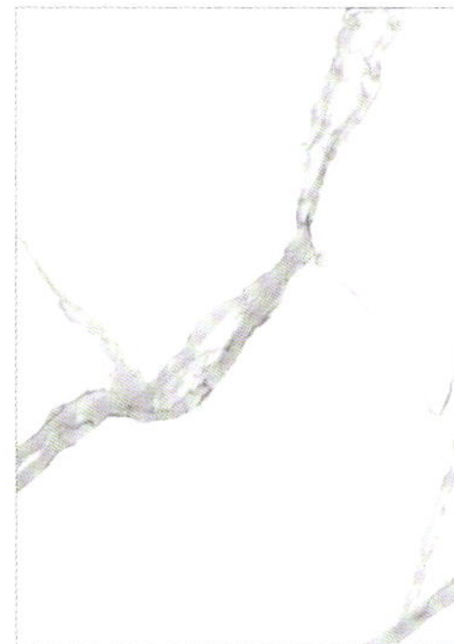

White Statutario marble

Custom-designed JLD rug by Diurne

Sand color stone

Jouve / Hematites-encrusted resin side table by Ado Chale from Yves Gastou, Paris / Curtains in Rubelli silk • **PHOTO 7** / Bronze and crystal chandelier "Lustre Gourmette" by Hervé Van der Straeten • **PHOTO 8** / Art piece by Michele Oka Doner / Custom-designed JLD plaster ruban stairs and railing / Ebony-stained oak • **PHOTO 9** / Pair of wall lights "Anneau" in bronze and Japanese paper by Hervé Van Der Straeten • **PHOTO 10** / Custom-designed JLD chandelier, lampshade by Anne Sokolsky / Custom-designed JLD stool upholstered with Perennial's terry toweling • **PHOTO 11** / Circular ceiling opening designed by JLD to mirror the circular rug / Custom-designed JLD rug based on a Japanese kimono motif by Diurne / Custom-designed JLD upholstered folding-screen headboard in Romo linen, Mokuba ruban and nail heads by Collection Pierre / Custom-made bed skirt in Romo linen/ Pair of bronze and black opaline gueridon reading lamps with tray by Maison Jansen / Pair of 1960s armchairs by Ramos covered in Romo / Wall fabric in horse hair by Le Crin, Paris / Glass and black-lacquered metal table lamp from Alain Demachy / Custom-designed JLD sofa / Bronze floor lamp by Philippe Hiquily / Wall sculpture by Curtis Jeer •

ASPEN
FALCON 2000

This twelve-seat Falcon 2000 was entirely refurbished, transforming a confined, generic and technical cabin into an intimate space with understanded luxury. Bringing an aesthetic and a comfort to travel, the idea was to play with textures, making reference to the materials and finishes used in the crafting of luxury travel goods. The jet's outside paint color and pattern were designed to match the interior palette of silver, camel, burgundy and a grey.

How did you approach the distribution of the space?

Inside the plane, I created three specific zones by designing a custom rug in an asymmetrical constructivist pattern to visually define the spaces. I wanted to avoid a repetitive floor pattern, which can create a long 'bowling alley' effect. At the head of the plane, the comfortable armchairs are covered in ivory-toned leather with taupe inserts and contrasting bordeaux piping to jazz it up a bit. Whereas it is customary to keep all the seating identical, I added variations, in terms of leather insert colors and piping, to the second and third groups of seats in order to break up the monotony of the carriage. The upper walls and windows were treated in a harlequin-stitched, ivory-toned suede. The lower walls are in woven burgundy leather straps. Instead of being polished, the wood is matte finished and so is all of the silver metal hardware, keeping a harmonious and comforting palette.

Airplane security regulations impose long and costly treatments to mixed and synthetic fabrics. What adjustments did you make?

The biggest challenge was adhering to the aviation rules governing the types of materials allowed. Luckily, materials that are 100 percent natural are considered plane-proof, which allowed me to use the same fabrics I regularly employ for my interior design projects.

You were inspired by the artisanal vocabulary of luxury leather goods.

It's all in the details. The leather is distressed with a patina much like the one on Italian shoes. It is also perforated, employing the detailing on driving gloves and the stitches found on travel bags.

The choice of colors was critical.

You have to pay a lot of attention to what to choose. In making my selection, it was important to source options that would be materially and visually soothing after a ten-hour flight. The ivory wall shade blends in during a daytime flight and has the added benefit, at night, of deflecting electric light so the cabin doesn't become overly bright.

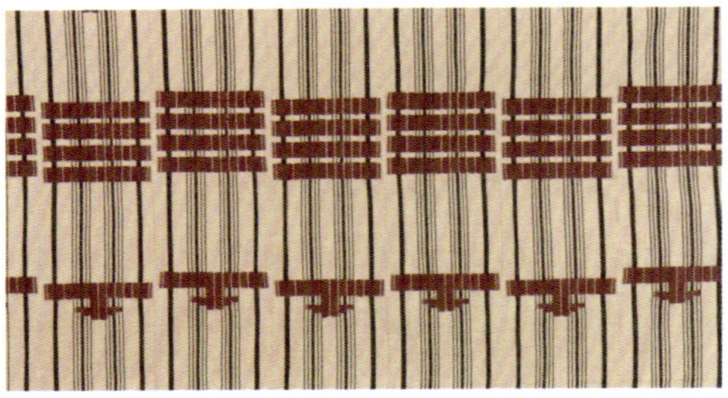

Hudson from Pierre Frey

Zimmer+Rohde

Perforated suede Eggshell

Custom-designed JLD rug by Tai Ping

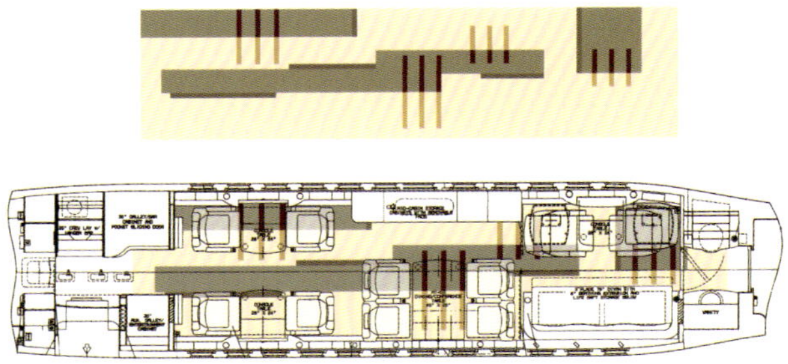

Custom-designed JLD rug by Tai Ping

PHOTO 2 / Custom-designed Jean-Louis Deniot rug, Constructivist-inspired pattern by Tai Ping / Brown leather Hermès briefcase • **PHOTO 3** / Walls upholstered in diamond-stitched ivory suede by Majilite / Ceiling covered in pearlized leather / Seat covered in Edelman Leather Dream cow / Taupe insert and piping by Edelman Leather / Woven burgundy leather straps by Garrett cover the lower walls • **PHOTO 4** / Custom-designed JLD back pillows and throw in baby alpaca by Alta Pampa, made in Argentina / Fumo glasses by Muriel Grateau / Matte white porcelain dish set by Muriel Grateau • **PHOTO 5** / Sofa covered in Les Météores initially designed by Ruhlmann for the Prelle / Accent pillow in Fontaine by

Gray beige grained leather

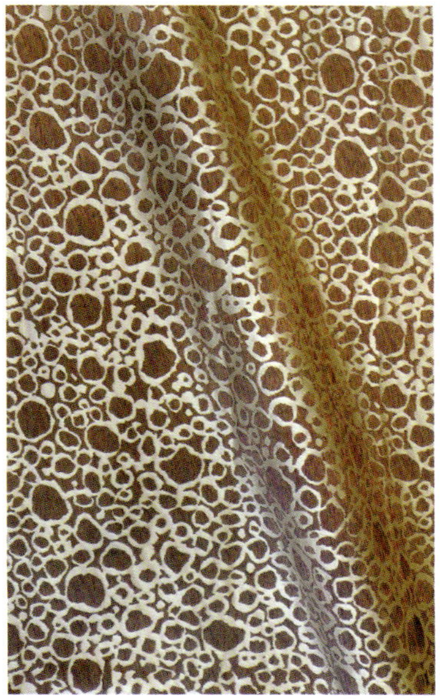
Ruhlmann fabric by Prelle

Embossed leather Stingray pattern

Burgundy braided leather

Diamond-stitched suede

Intermezzo tea set by Muriel Grateau

Le Manach / Accent pillow in Castor by Antoine d'Albiousse (formerly Destombes) / Throw on sofa in baby alpaca and silk by Alta Pampa / Vintage Danish vase / Black mother-of-pearl ashtray by R&Y Augousti / Stingray box by R&Y Augousti • **PHOTO 6** / Leather embossed in a stingray pattern and glazed to accentuate the texture / Burl wood stained chocolate brown with a matte finish varnish • **PHOTO 7** / Bedsheets custom-embroidered reference "Frontières" by Vis-à-Vis / Baby alpaca bedspread by Alta Pampa / Accent pillow with Zimmer+Rohde / Mohair velvet accent pillow in Brunschwig & Fils •

LONDON
EATON SQUARE

Eaton Square is situated in London's exclusive Belgravia district. Constructed in the early nineteenth century, it is the largest square in the city and its adjoining buildings, historic parks, and gardens have been registered as landmarks. It's an iconic address representing English tradition, with an interior architecture combining French, British and colonial elements that create an understated elegance.

If there is one address in London, it's Eaton Square...

Yes, and it's why I felt the project itself didn't need to try too hard. It feels elaborate, sophisticated, and at the same time easy and unfussy, bringing the right balance between historical references and eclectic juxtapositions. With such a high-profile project, it was also important to infuse a dose of humility into an apartment that otherwise would be rather grand.

What were the challenges of this project?

Normally, in this historic area, you cannot connect spaces horizontally. You are expected to respect the skeleton and the archetype of these protected buildings, which were constructed vertically. In this specific instance, we were able to develop the project horizontally because it brought together three apartments in several buildings. When you expand a space horizontally you create more square footage, but it doesn't mean you generate more light. The real challenge was seizing and redistributing the light through the entire 4,500-square-foot space.

You created a very different floor plan...

Yes. We literally demolished everything, allowing us to create perfectly symmetrical plans, a rarity in England. The English and French floor plans generate very different flows, one separates the rooms into enclosed private areas, whereas the other opens them up and connects them.

I included as many double doors as in a typical French layout to recreate structural symmetry, visual balance, and easy access. At almost thirteen feet in height, the doors reach the ceiling and open up the space, giving more modern proportions to the rooms. They are placed facing the windows so one is always walking toward the light. And they are worked with reflective surfaces of inlayed horsehair or mirror treatments to illuminate the living areas.

Photography by Stephan Julliard

PARIS IN THE 1920s

PARIS IN THE 1920s

FRENCH
FRENCH STYLE

ASTON MARTIN
GREEN
GREEN
LOUIS VUITTON
LIVING IN STYLE PARIS
JANSEN
CHANEL
AFRICA
London
CALATRAVA
HOTEL STORIES
ASPEN

What details allowed you to create a fluid narrative?

Sometimes just a simple ceiling molding allowed me to carry through a design vocabulary referencing both the Palladian architectural style prevalent in seventeenth- and eighteenth-century England and French Art Déco from the 1920s. Custom designed, the profiles are cubist in shape, creating the impression of classical molding; but they are actually geometric in a sleek neoclassical silhouette. Most of the detailing was dictated by structural limitations. For example, the coffered ceiling in the dining room was designed to hide one of the concrete beams.

Which room really shines your signature?

The living room because it has every period represented, really. There are a pair of *meubles d'appui* like you would have in a classical eighteenth-century room, except they're in parchment with a black trim. You have the graphic 1940s black-lacquer Dominic chair in a burst of yellow velvet that lights up the room. The sofa seems classical but it's a design I did for George Smith. For a playful accent, I placed a bright gold Hubert le Gall chandelier in the center of the room.

Yellow is not a color you use often.

As it is the ground floor and there is lack of direct sunlight, it was important to choose luminous colors. The role of the yellow was to bring rays of sunlight into an otherwise somber room. I also used iridescent grey paint to bring warmth and give off a luminous effect.

NAPOLÉON

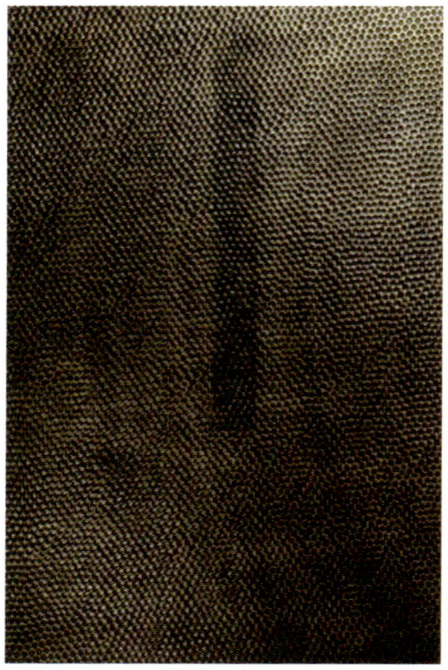
Black-patinated hammered brass

Parchment

Back-painted glass by Forence Girette

Custom-designed JLD bench

Blond mahogany

Interior door sample

PHOTO 1 / Pair of wooden stools in braided leather by Naturtex / Pair of Scarabées wall lights by Hamilton Conte / Hanging lantern by Circa Lighting • **PHOTO 2** / Large area rug with rounded edges by Ferreira de Sá / Custom-designed JLD coffee table with hammered, patinated brass / Heather sofa by JLD for Georges Smith London in Scion Living and Kvadrat / Set of cushions in Pasaya, Calucci and Romo, Houlès piping / Pair of vintage armchairs by Raphaël in Brochier yellow velvet / Chandelier by Hubert le Gall • **PHOTO 4** / Pair of alabaster globes by Alain Ellouz / Pair of custom-designed JLD cabinets in parchment and ebonized wood • **PHOTO 5** / Pair of vintage table lamps and lampshades by Anne Sokolsky / Heather sofa by JLD for Georges Smith in Scion Living and Kvadrat / South African wall art • **PHOTO 6** / Pair of stools by Hamilton Conte covered in Colefax & Fowler / Fireplace in back-painted glass by Florence Girette and bronze trim by Maison Schmit / French Regency gilded mirror • **PHOTO 7** / Mid-century desk lamp / Custom-designed JLD black-lacquered wood desk / Desk chair by JLD for Georges Smith in Jab / Rug by Lesage / Italian 1960s chandelier / Coffee table by Hervé Van Der Straeten • **PHOTO 8** / Wall painted by Florence Girette / Set of four wall lights by Hamilton Conte / Large custom-designed JLD patinated-brass dining table with back-painted gloss top / Louis XV French antique chandelier • **PHOTO 9** / Painted canvas wallcovering by Florence Girette / Egg lantern by Hervé Van Der Straeten / Bench by JLD for Marc de Berny / Alexander Calder tapestry • **PHOTO 10** / Custom-designed JLD stair railing / Bench by JLD for Marc de Berny • **PHOTO 11** / Wallpaper by Arte /

Painted canvas wallcovering

Iridescent wall paint

Horsehair sandwiched glass

Custom-woven fabric

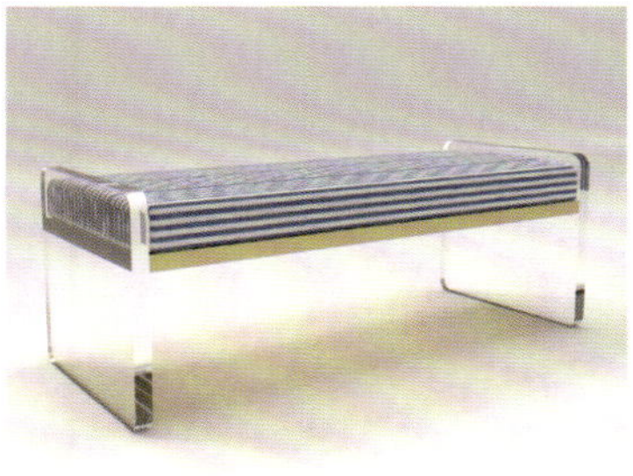

Custom-designed JLD acrylic and brass bench

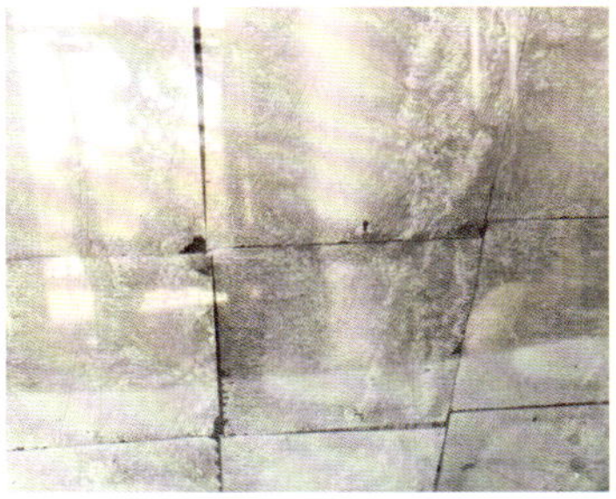

Silver leaf behind glass

Custom-designed JLD sofa in Jules et Jim / Set of cushions in Romo, Jab, Jane Churchill, and Pierre Frey / Custom-designed JLD ceramic table lamp / Roman blinds in Jules et Jim / Vintage mirror • **PHOTO 12** / Custom-designed JLD set of eight dining chairs in Jules et Jim / Pair of wall lights by Circa Lighting / 1960s forged-iron-and-alabaster / Custom-designed JLD table • **PHOTO 13** / Set of four barstools by Phase Design covered in Romo / Set of three glass-and-alabaster hanging lights by Lee Broom • **PHOTOS 14 & 15** / Chair by Hamilton Conte in Jim Thompson and Métaphores / Cushion in Rubelli / Set of four wall lights by Drummonds / Okulus mirror by JLD for Marc de Berny / Roman blinds in Jules et Jim and Colefax & Fowler • **PHOTO 16** / Wall in James Malone / Area rug in New Zealand wool by Esti / Pair of custom-designed JLD gray-lacquered nightstands / Vintage pair of crystal table lamps / Lalique chandelier / Custom-designed JLD headboard in Kirkby Design / Custom-designed JLD bench in James Malone fabric • **PHOTO 17** / Custom-designed JLD lacquered-steel bed / Custom-designed JLD bench upholstered in Pasaya / Custom-designed JLD nightstand in blackened wood and parchment / Pair of customed-designed JLD brass double table lamps / Vintage 1960s mirror • **PHOTO 18** / Antique marble Napoleon bust by Canova / Custom-designed JLD triangle mirror / Vintage sculpture by Curtis Jeer • **PHOTO 19** / JLD matte-lacquered vanity and travertine top / Custom-designed JLD shagreen mirror / Vintage 1950s wall lights / Nineteenth-century bronze bust •

NORMANDY
DACHA

Finished in 1883, the Château Gabriel is a neo-Gothic nineteenth-century villa of traditional Normand design that sits on a 75-acre wooded property near the seaside resort of Deauville. A century later, in 1983, Pierre Bergé and Yves Saint Laurent acquired the property and grounds and commissioned Jacques Grange to transform them in a nineteenth-century Napoleon III decorative theme where Marcel Proust's *A la recherche du temps perdu* is the central inspiration. On the vast estate grounds they built a small dacha, a Russian country cottage, which has now been entirely renovated.

First imagined by Yves Saint Laurent, the Russian dacha is but a short walk from the main house.

Yes, it's like the cabana in the woods! It's, actually a small compound of several independent spaces. The main lodge consists of one large room with a kitchen and guest bathroom. There are two other smaller chalets, each with a guest suite. In addition, a vintage Gypsy trailer was transformed into a guest bedroom with a dressing area and bath.

The idea was never to faithfully recreate a Russian wood cabin but instead to suggest the backdrop of a romanticized narrative. This allowed for the space and the choice of furniture to be more evocative and open to storytelling.

Today, the current owners are Russian. Did they have any specific requests?

They asked me not to fall into too much exoticism. They were not looking for the perfect historical reconstitution of a Russian dacha but a contemporary translation to really make their own.

I felt very respectful of the place, its DNA and its initial purpose were to be more of a smoking room for Yves Saint Laurent. I also felt free to explore different options because there was no real starting point. It was like a blank page. Originally, the dacha referenced a winter white Russia, whereas I amplified elements that were inspired by the proximity of the seaside.

The main lodge is one large open room.

It was important to initially position every element because the space itself is perfectly symmetrical.

Photography by Stephan Julliard

There's a moment where you need to respect the symmetry, but also to counter it in order to create a rhythm and avoid repetition. For me, there's an element of magic in bringing together the multitude of individual components to create a coherent and flawless ensemble.

What was your approach?

The common thread was to play with surfaces, colors, textures, and patterns on various scales and complexities to achieve a visual depth and harmony. Most of the content used is not Russian, but Austrian and Turkish, mixed with custom-designed pieces.

From the micro texture to the XXL pattern, I felt very comfortable with a maximalist approach to every treatment. The challenge was to find balance in the juxtapositions, making sure that one didn't override the other, while still having elements that popped without creating a cacophony. We shopped for antique fabrics and layered them as appliqués to create a sense of intensity and richness. Because of the numerous textures the whole place is extremely tactile. The chairs, for example, have eight different fabric layers appliquéd. Nonetheless, it doesn't mean the place looks extremely busy. Other pieces I designed include the main sofa, inspired by the model owned by Russian ballet icon Rudolf Nureyev, who was friends of the Bergé–Saint Laurent couple.

You designed an impressive chandelier for the main room...

In a neo-Gothic style, inspired by the work of nineteenth-century Russian architect Ivan Ropet, the chandelier acts as the anchor for the room. Requiring the most work, it's a massive object: six-and-a-half-feet high by nearly four feet in diameter, it was designed entirely by computer in 3D. It was then carved out of wood, casted in bronze, and enameled. It's like a pendulum in the middle of the room that grounds the entire space. Setting the tone, the fireplace I redesigned is on a larger scale to create a giant Russian stove echoing the same blue color palette that recalls the sea.

What attracts you to institutional projects?

I love working on projects that can be considered institutional, according to their strong history or iconic status, because it's another way to challenge myself. What can scare some people makes me want to tackle this kind of subject even more. In my own work, I systematically take into consideration the past, and then detach it and fast forward it into the future, which explains why working on historical projects comes naturally to me. It's about disappearing behind the exercise and finding the right visual vocabulary to write a contemporary narrative specific to each institution.

Fossilized wood top

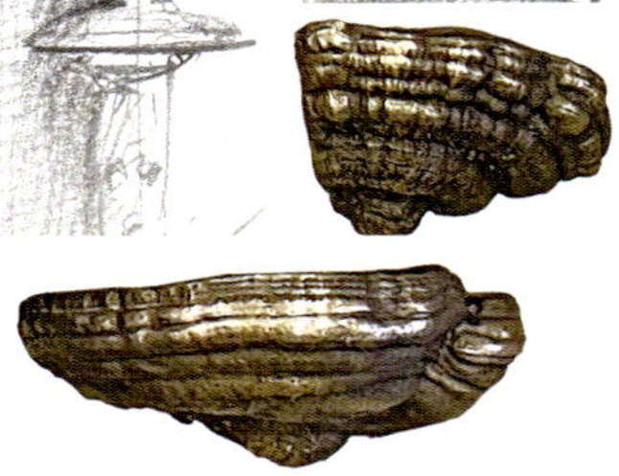

Casted bronze brackets

Birch veneer

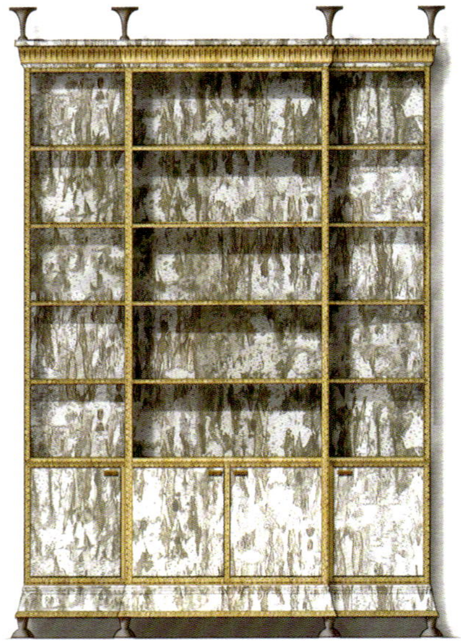

Custom-designed JLD bookcase

Volga Bleu Drapeau by Pierre Frey

Glazed ceramic custom stove

PHOTO 2 / Set of 1950s cement outdoor furniture / Pair of cement planters • **PHOTO 3** / 1920s armchairs and ottoman by Etienne Kolhmann covered in Décors Barbares, Fortuny and Filippo Uecher, Houlès and Mokuba piping • **PHOTO 4** / Jean-Louis Deniot custom-designed daybed of carved white sycamore, carved and brass decorative details upholstered in Filippo Uecher, Houlès trimmings / Pair of 17th-century embroidery-mounted cushions on Loro Piana cashmere / Custom-designed JLD sofa covered in Brochier, ribbon and fringe by Houlès and Dedar / Set of cushions in Décors Barbares and Fortuny, Houlès and IDF piping / Nineteenth-century gilded mirror frame / 1940s French roster tapestry by Jean Lurçat / Three custom-designed JLD coffee tables with petrified wood tops on custom-casted bronze bases • **PHOTO 5** / Russian-style dining set / Tablecloth in Antoine d'Albiousse and Casamance, Houlès trims / Custom-designed JLD bookshelves clad with birchwood veneer / Custom-designed JLD Hugh chandelier in bronze ropes, crystal glass and enameled to pay homage to architect Ivan Ropet • **PHOTO 6** / Pair of nineteenth-century sleeper chairs upholstered in Décors Barbares, Fortuny and Le Manach, Houlès piping / Set of eight 3D-printed, custom-designed JLD stained, sandblasted pin shelves / Set of nine antique samovars / Ceramic stove designed by JLD, by Nikolai Koshelev / Bronze-casted mushroom shelves for traditional Russian fashion figurines • **PHOTO 7** / Nineteenth-century Russian chair / Empire-style floor lamp and lampshade in Décors Barbares by Anne Sokolsky • **PHOTO 8** / 1900s gramophone / Malachite nineteenth-century accessories • **PHOTO 9** / Art Nouveau wooden bench / Nineteenth-century lantern / Circa 1900

Custom-designed JLD chandelier in bronze, enameled and blown glass

Custom-designed JLD rug by Diurne

Plumette in blue & gold by Fortuny

Sycamore carved sled daybed

Barbotine vase / Curtain fabric by Le Manach • **PHOTO 10** / Pair of vintage rare hand-painted enameled gold leaf benches reupholstered in Pierre Frey, Houlès piping / Large enameled Art Nouveau ceramic column and urn by C. Massier • **PHOTO 11** / Pair of Russian wooden carved armchairs with cushions in Fortuny / Marble and semi-precious stone marquetry top an Art Nouveau iron-leg base • **PHOTO 12** / Vintage rug / Early 1900s Arts & Crafts pendant brass-and-glass light lantern / Custom-designed JLD canopy and Russian wooden bed in Raoul Textiles and Décors Barbares / Bedcover in Holland & Sherry and Décors Barbares, nineteenth-century vintage lace / Cushions in Filippo Uecher and Fortuny • **PHOTO 14** / 1900s Medieval-style curule upholstered in Mark Alexander and Décors Barbares • **PHOTO 15** / Art Nouveau candle lantern by Baccarat / Art Deco metal mirror by Paul Kiss • **PHOTO 16** / Art Nouveau lamp by Degué / *Blue Hydrangeas*, 1970s tapestry by Bernard Buffet / 1900s bronze pendulum / Bronze Dutch desk set in cloisonné technique circa late 1800s / Metal-and-glass mirror by Lemanceau • **PHOTO 18** / 1940s pair of table lamps and lampshades in Décors Barbares by Anne Sokolsky / Pair of curtains in Décors Barbares, Mokuba piping / Bedcover in Jennifer Shorto and Tissus Tartares, Houlès piping / Pair of cushions in Fortuny and Décors Barbares, Houlès piping / Pair of nightstands covered with Décors Barbares / Mirror by Alfonse Giroux • **PHOTO 19** / 1930s vintage wooden stool covered in Braquenié / Napoleon III–style mirror / English Art Nouveau armchair covered in Le Manach and Tissus Tartares / 1900s secretary • **PHOTO 20** / Art Deco mirror in hammered wrought iron with custom-made shades •

MONTFORT-L'AMAURY
FRANCE

Historic buildings never cease to evolve and this sixteenth-century tower in the French medieval town of Montfort l'Almaury, just twenty miles from Paris, is a case in point. The challenge was to preserve the existing construction and to create a modern addition that flawlessly juxtaposes the past and present. The owner asked for one thing: no gratuitous architectural design.

What is different when approaching a historical project?

The main issue to resolve with this structure was to create fluidity within the several floors of open spaces stacked one on top of another. It's quite complicated technically to assign specific functionalities to large individual rooms that historically were multipurpose.

Without breaking up the original volume, we began by cutting the full height of the three-floor tower in half and then pushing back the facade by about sixteen feet. To double the size of the original sixteenth-century space, we used historical antique beams, floors, and doors while adding contemporary comforts.

The client brief was very specific.

Yes, it's made for a great Frenchman who is not only a passionate adventurer but also a horse aficionado. When he hired me, he was very clear that he didn't want the space to feel decorated, and insisted every design decision be justified. No gratuitous acts were allowed. From the onset, he wanted to push the limitations both technically and esthetically and asked me to limit the number of pieces used to a bare minimum.

Photography by Christoph Theurer

How did you resolve the challenge?

By playing with the confrontation of various historical periods, I reworked classic furniture pieces to give a sense of excitement without resonating as formal. In the library, there is an nineteenth-century *canapé* that I completely dismantled and updated by giving it the curved shape of a 1970s Italian sofa. I included Austrian pieces from 1900 mixed with 1960 designs from Los Angeles, seventeenth-century Dutch objects with brutalist lamps from the 1970s. Each element was seamlessly woven into a larger picture of continuity through time. By introducing a stylistic eclecticism, I wanted to make a connection, a bridge creating dialogues between the elements.

What surprised you about this approach?

I realized that even by using fifty percent fewer pieces in a room, it can still feel as furnished and as vibrant as if there were twice as many. I learned how to say the exact same thing, but with far fewer components.

Did you compose the rooms differently?

The layout had to respect the long history of the edifice but also needed to be oriented to the twenty-first century. Consequently, it was a looser, more low-key plan, which introduced an informal flow in the room. However, when you try to have a more open plan using historical pieces it's complicated because they can act like obstacles. We tend to place classical furniture free-standing in rooms, but originally, they were set against the walls which is why they all have flat backs.

How did you achieve the fluidity between time and space?

As I was limited by the amount of furniture in each room, I introduced a layer of depth, texture, and substance on the walls. Like a blanket or a unique backdrop, each zone had its own made-to-measure colored wall stucco patina that softened the room, creating a warm and relaxed atmosphere. It was a great way to appropriate and embody the space without making it look decorated.

Abstract painted forest mural by M. Kiss

Custom-designed JLD rug by Diurne

Reclaimed seventeenth-century beams

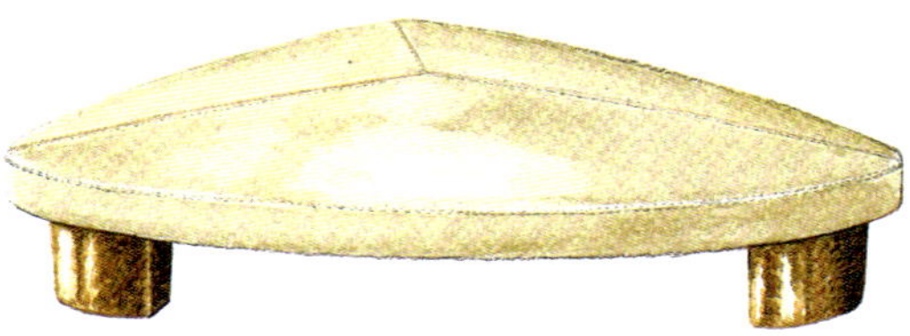

Custom-designed JLD ottoman

Distressed grey leather

Seventeenth-century reclaimed stone floor

PHOTO 1 / Custom-designed Jean-Louis Deniot dining console table / Dining chairs by Sido and François Thevenin / Vintage bronze brutalist ceiling light / Seventeenth-century ebony cabinet / Seventeenth-century painting of royal feast scene • **PHOTO 2** / Custom-designed JLD ottoman in leather / Danish wingback armchair upholstered in Bisson Bruneel / Pair of large wrought iron and bronze andirons by Raymond Subes / Italian sculpted wood floor lamp by Anne Sokolsky / Pair of large sculptural pitchers by Annick Lodereau / Marble abstract sculpture by Van Loocke / Louis XIV-style curule stool • **PHOTO 3** / Custom-designed JLD curved sofa upholstered with Sanderson / Set of cushions in Fortuny, Élitis and Sanderson, Edmond Petit / Acid-patina vintage metal end table / Leather lamp designed by Etienne Kohlmann / Louis XIV-style gold-leaf wood game table / Vintage fossilized wood coffee table / Abstract painting by Martin Verdet / Ceiling light by Niamh Barry • **PHOTO 4** / Ceiling light by Hubert le Gall / Custom-designed JLD area rug by Solstys / Set of three bronze coffee tables with stone tops from Galerie Negropontes / Impressive collection of 80 Victorian period mirrors from the Paris flea market • **PHOTO 5** / Mid-century parchment table with four 1960s Danish barrel chairs / Eighteenth-century baroque gilt-wood mirror / 1970s petrified wood lamp by Willy Daro / Curtains in Brochier • **PHOTO 6** / Custom-designed JLD sofa upholstered in Bisson Bruneel / Set of cushions in Rubelli and Jennifer Shorto / Fake-fur throw by Pierre Frey / Sculptural two-tiered ceramic lamp / Curtains in Sabina Fay Braxton / Pair of nineteenth-century bronze candelabras • **PHOTO 8** / Wingback bergère marquise by Jansen in Kvadrat and Houlès piping / Floor lamp by Carl Aubock • **PHOTO 9** / Regency-period armchair covered in Fortuny • **PHOTO 10** / Seventeenth-century two-part cupboard / Nineteenth-century gold leaf and

Textured and ombré wall stucco

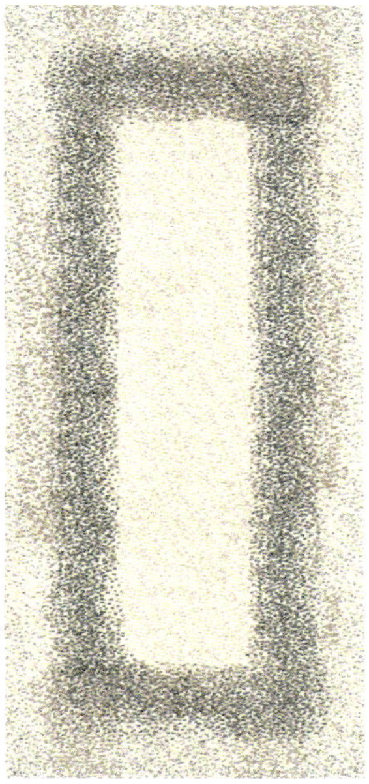

Custom-designed JLD rug by Diurne

Custom-designed JLD medieval-style bed

Eighteenth-century antique floor planks

Sheepskin

blackened carved wood mirror / 1960s Venini egg light / Seventeenth-century chair upholstered with Pasaya and Zimmer+Rohde • **PHOTO 11** / Bronze bamboo curved vanity table from Maison Ramsey / Napoleon III-period blackened wood with intricate inlaid-bone décor chair upholstered with blue-grey velvet / Triptyque table mirror by Gilbert Poillerat / Chandelier bronze Art Nouveau style / Curtains in Sabina Fay Bratxon • **PHOTO 12** / Seventeenth-century Chinese octagonal wood table / Large 1960s stoneware vase / Bronze abstract sculpture by Stefan Christensen / Ceiling light by Atelier Rick Tegelaar • **PHOTO 13** / Custom-designed rug by Diunre / Mid-century teardrop-shaped wall light / Art Déco style wingback armchair and ottoman upholstered in Nobilis / Twist shelf by Carol Egan from Galerie BSL • **PHOTO 14** / Custom-designed JLD bed canopy upholstered with Lelièvre, Houlès and Mokuba piping / Pair of 1960s glass hanging lanterns / Pair of curtains in Rubelli / Custom-designed JLD bronze bench / Pair of 1960s Italian commodes / Pair of bedside table lamps by Mathilde Pénicaud • **PHOTO 15** / Pair of curtains in Donghia fabric / Custom-designed JLD 'antique' mirror with integrated lightings / Nineteenth-century rosewood armchair upholstered in de Le Cuona / Mauritanian area rug • **PHOTO 16** / Brass counter weight ceiling light by Florian Schulz / Lounge chair and ottoman by Ico Parisi / Abstract painting by Martin Verdet / Seventeenth-century Flemish cabinet • **PHOTO 17** Pair of armchairs by Sido and François Thevenin / Seventeenth-century monastery table used as a desk • **PHOTO 18** / Vintage 1960s long billiards-style ceiling light / Set of gilded Regency chairs upholstered with Japanese Genshedo fabric and Métaphores bouclette / Candelsticks by Astier de Villatte / Nineteenth-century blue-and-white china / Roman blind cotton by Jennifer Shorto •

ÎLE DE RÉ
FRANCE

Off the north coast of France, Île de Ré is a much sought-after seaside destination receiving almost as many hours of sunshine as the French Riviera. Luminous and radiant, this beautiful family home from the 1940s was built like a model hacienda and renovated with painstaking integrity. For this child-oriented project, the narrative of the interiors had a fixed objective: to mark their visual senses and foster future childhood memories.

This is a very personal project...

It is a house I designed for my nieces and nephews. I imagined a picture-perfect backdrop for them to explore and create wonderful childhood memories. It was really the expression of the "happy family at the beach" in a very retro kind of a way. I wanted to spark their emotions and give them something by which to remember this period of their lives.

What components did you use to achieve this effect?

The whole house is white, and I used primary blues with a touch of red and yellow to achieve a cinematographic feel. With such a restrained palette, I wanted to give the impression of a comic book universe with very graphic defined shapes and colors.

My sister liked the Josef Frank fabrics that I used as visual punctuations throughout the house. As chance would have it, I received a container full of furniture from California and was able to fully furnish the house in mid-century American furniture. It naturally gave it a surf vibe. I introduced neo-Gothic chairs and plaster wall lights, which for me, referenced 1940s fairy tales and movie theaters.

Photography by Stephan Julliard

Keeping the integrity of the house was important to you.

I wanted to restore the purity and freshness of the original. In order to keep the authenticity of the house, I duplicated the few remaining antique doors throughout and also created the kitchen cabinetry to match. The ceiling moldings were identically recreated as if they had been made in the 1940s just like the millwork in the bathrooms and all of the crackled and glazed tiling.

How did you bring the water element into the décor?

In the entrance hall, all the steps were in white, matching the walls and creating a very linear appearance. I thought why not read it as a vertical, almost like a wall. At first glance, you don't see it as being three dimensional. I commissioned an artist to create a painted canvas on the theme of water and to use the stair risers as a full ornamental panel.

You had a "sandstorm" wall treatment in one of the rooms...

I like to give a theme to each room. For this bedroom that was entirely white on white, I felt a change in the color scheme would enhance the space and allow me to include a reference to sand; after all, we're on an island. The shape of the room is triangular—and to break up this geometry the loose geometric pattern became a type of sandstorm.

Was the process of designing for children very different?

In a vacation home, it's not about making the most spacious children's rooms. It's about making a space that is super flexible so that playtime with friends and sleepovers are possible. There is enough room to respect each other's privacy, but at the same time it's thought out for maximum capacity and summer fun.

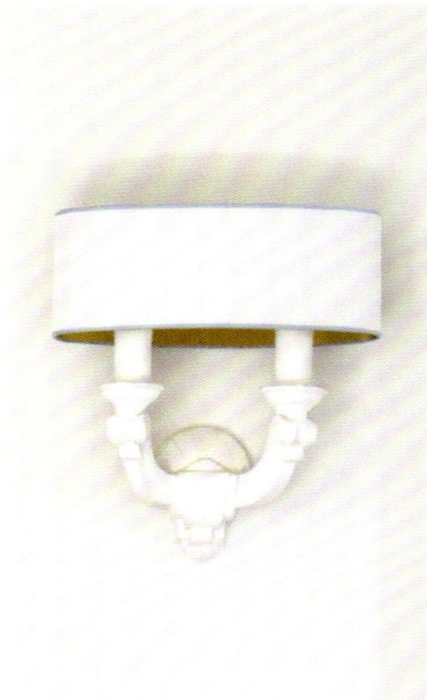

Vintage plaster wall lamp

Pierre Frey fabrics

Wall painting by Florence Girette

Blue "Majorelle" paint

Reissue Josef Frank, Primavera by Svenskt Tenn

Artisanal textile from Tangier

Sisal rope casings

PHOTO 2 / Decorative paint effect simulating sea foam / Vintage 1950s globe found in Los Angeles • **PHOTO 3** / Curule 1940s armchairs in Livio de Simone / Textured plaster walls / French limestone grey and sand / Set of 1940s plaster theater wall lights, lampshades by Anne Sokolsky / 1950s bamboo sideboard / Custom-designed Jean-Louis Deniot bone mirror frame / Wooden model of the sailboat *America* by François Boyer •.**PHOTO 4** / Vintage armchairs from Christopher Gibbs in custom-woven stripe from Tangier / 1950s coffee table in the shape of a diving board in exotic wood, from Los Angeles / Custom-designed JLD plaster mantel fireplace with vintage French 1940s andirons / Fish sculpture by Ernie Abdelnour / Two vintage marine lanterns / Mid-century decorative glassware • **PHOTO 5** / Moroccan rug from Marrakech / Neo-Gothic 1940s painted bamboo dining chairs upholstered with fabric from Tangier / Custom-designed JLD banquette in glazed "Primavera" by Josef Frank / Custom-designed JLD table with distressed gold leaf and hammered iron and ash-gray stained-oak top / Danish 1950s ceramic candlesticks / Sconces by Audoux Minet / Rafia wallpaper by Au fil des Couleurs / French limestone / Artworks by Frédéric de Luca • **PHOTO 6** / Neo-Gothic 1940s iron box / Sofa designed by JLD for Georges Smith Kirky design, Iona fabrics / Set of cushions in Iona and "Grona Faglar" by Josef Frank / Vintage Jean Prouvé-style oak sideboard / Mid-century teak floor lamp by Jean Rispal • **PHOTO 7** / Custom-designed JLD mattress sofa "Notturno" by Josef Frank / Nesting table and floor lamp by Audoux Minet / Custom-designed JLD Roman blind in "Notturno" by Josef Frank / Vintage Moroccan rug / Mid-century Scandinavian desk by Peter Lovig Nielsen / 1940s forged-iron curule in Linen by Romo / Vintage lamp with custom wicker lampshade / Double door with custom JLD rope casing / Photography Slim Aarons • **PHOTO 8** / Custom-designed JLD double pillow stool • **PHOTO 9** / Custom-made bedspread / Vintage 1950s storage headboard from Los Angeles / Storm paint effect by Florence Girette / Vintage papier-mâché moon mirror /

Bamboo

Painting by Florence Girette

Custom-designed JLD plaster fireplace

Moroccan wool rug

Reissue Josef Frank "Notturno" by Svenskt Tenn

Vintage wicker lamp with marine shade / Sandstone vintage lamps with lampshades by Anne Sokolsky / 1940s fish bones painting • **PHOTO 10** / Custom-designed JLD kitchen cabinet based on reclaimed 1940s double-door profiles with antique mirror insert / Grey limestone and Zimbabwe granite / Vintage Arlus wall light / 1940s rope donkey head sculpture • **PHOTO 11** / Vintage 1950s bamboo chair / Custom-designed JLD cabinet with antique mirror inset / Flamed and brushed Zimbabwe granite top / Curtains in "mousse original" by Robert Normand / Roman blind in Romo linen / French 1940s portrait, Anonymous • **PHOTO 12** / Vintage 1950s bamboo chair / Custom-design JLD antique brass wall lights / Custom-designed JLD painted-wood built-in shelves / Vintage vases / Mirrors by Audoux Minet / Rope door stop by Williams-Sonoma • **PHOTO 13** / Custom-designed JLD bedspread in Tangier / Custom-designed JLD crochet bed canopy / Wallpaper by Thibaut / Custom-designed JLD nightstand with lamp / 1960s rattan and oak chest of drawers / Vintage 1970s ceramic obelisk lamp / Vintage 1950s chair covered in Romo linen / Curtains custom woven in Tangier / Painting by Erick Valencourt • **PHOTO 14** / Custom-designed JLD cabinet with Carrara marble top / Custom-designed JLD lacquered blue-painted metal-frame wall light / Custom-designed JLD mirror in a bone mosaic frame / Custom-designed JLD fish-scale crackled ceramic tiles • **PHOTO 15** / Custom-designed JLD vanity with Carrara marble top / Custom-designed JLD lacquered painted-yellow metal frame wall light / Custom-designed JLD mirror antique silver finish / Custom-designed JLD crackled ceramic wall tiles / Hudson Reed tubs • **PHOTO 16** / Custom-made wood-frame drawer bed with ceramic pulls from Anthropologie / Custom-made pom-pom bedspread from Tangier / Danish armchair by Hartmut Lohmeyer in Romo linen / Custom-designed JLD curtains in three different colors of neoprene fabric by Pierre Frey /Custom-designed JLD bean-shaped mirror / Wallpaper "My Terrazza" by Eno Studio / Rope donkey from Morocco •

PORTO VECCHIO
CORSICA

On the island of Corsica, this sprawling multileveled estate with stunning views of the Mediterranean blends in perfectly with the dense vegetation of the native scrub. Situated between sea and mountains, the local landscape served as the inspiration for the interiors of this villa situated near Porto-Vecchio.

The client's brief included the need for ample wall space to hang works from his art collection, lots of natural light, and guest quarters separate from the primary suite. He also wanted to incorporate pieces from his vast twentieth-century furniture collection by Pierre Jeanneret, Charlotte Perriand, and Jean Prouvé.

How did this location inspire you?

For me, it's extremely important that a place belongs to its setting, which is why I travel to each destination. Having spent many childhood holidays in Corsica, I already knew the island really well. Overrun by nature, the island always gives off a strong smell of maquis, the wild local vegetation that gives off the most exquisite scent. It's gorgeous.

Because of the wild and arid environment, I introduced a more brutalist design in this house and worked on rougher finishes with a controlled sense of rusticity. The starting point was a *bergerie*, the local sheep shed that is found in the Corsican mountains.

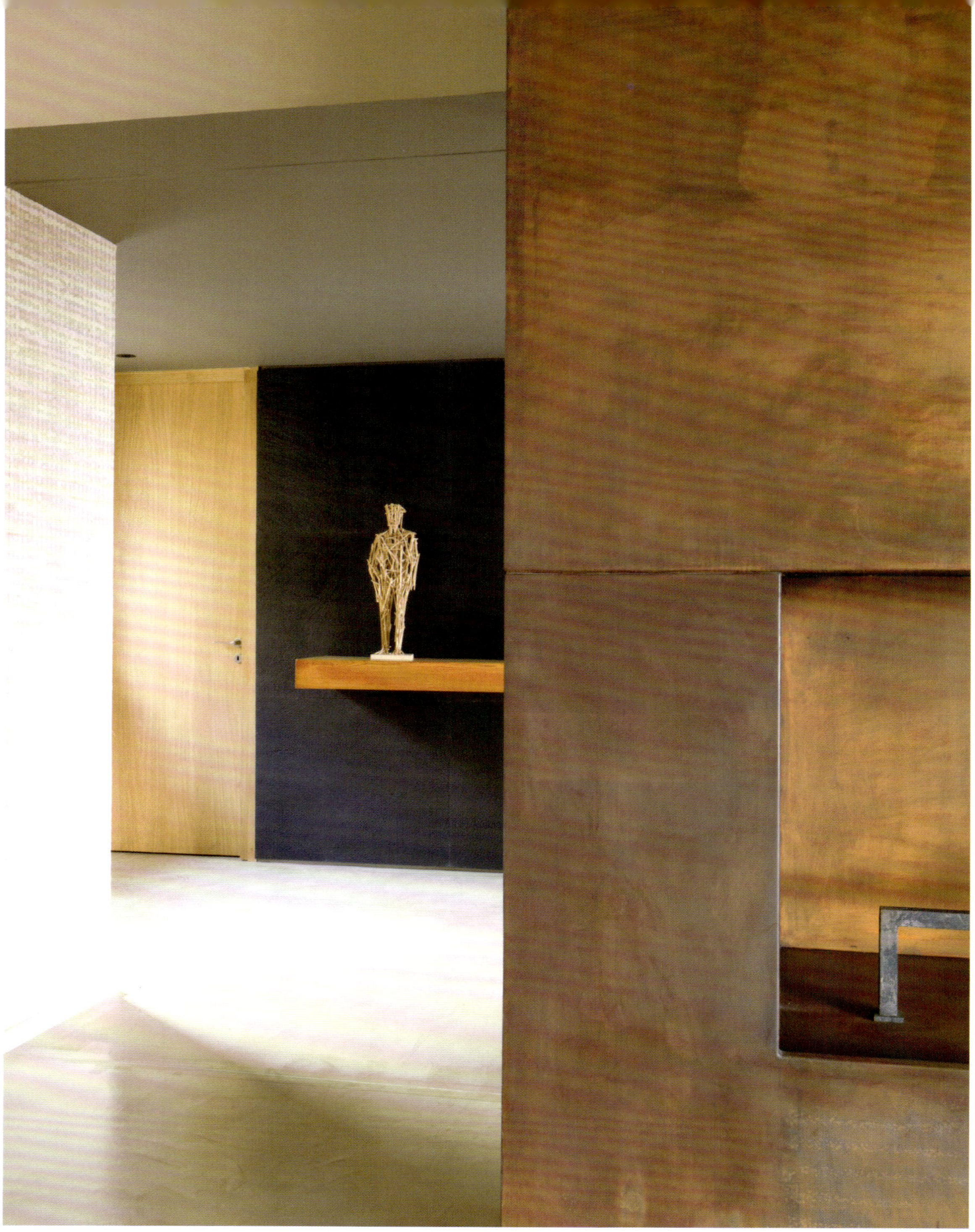

Creating dialogues is very important to you.

My design is linked to the local roots of each project without being forced. It should never feel out of context or overdone. All my projects are conceived, designed, and elaborated in Paris, but because I spend quite a bit of time on the architecture, it allows me to develop the perfect structural base. The content naturally follows from there. I think sustainable design is timeless because when it suits the property, it can span time. I treat each property like its own sculpture where eventually the content can change. For this project, the house was built on different levels. We placed the reception rooms and pool deck on the upper level with the primary bedroom suite. The guest bedrooms are separated down below with their own access and private gardens.

You are always open to working with local materials and techniques.

I introduced natural materials to soften the interiors and worked with the local stone, the lauze, which is a lovely color, a mix of gray, rust and green with a touch of blue. I also used the tones of the local soil for the sofa palettes.

In the interior, I wanted to avoid any reverberant surface and chose to give a really buffed and muted tone throughout. The shade of green is that of the local olives, the gray for the beams is inspired from the bark of the olive tree.

The flooring has an unexpected connection to Gabrielle Chanel...

To give a seamless experience between the outside and inside space, I chose a cement floor, but the owner, a serious collector, didn't want the house to look like a contemporary art gallery. I remembered a suede sofa that Coco Chanel had in her rue Cambon apartment in a color she referred to as "wet sand." It inspired me to do a wet sand-colored cement flooring throughout the entire property.

What was the inspiration behind the painted ceiling?

I commissioned Florence Girette to paint the entire vaulted ceiling inspired by the color of the local *lauze* stone, giving the space a more mineral feel, closer to the Corsican *bergeries* that were my initial inspirations. The dining room feels furnished at human height, but not overly busy. A low bookcase, made from raw oak, allows the owner to display pieces from his art collection. I placed the Jean Prouvé dining table diagonally, otherwise it would have looked too much like a canteen. Above it, we used a mobile piece by French contemporary artist Xavier Veihlan. Its counterweights regulate the height and allow you to lift it up or down. The mobile echoes very well with the Oswald Haerdtl chandelier from the 1950s in the adjoining room.

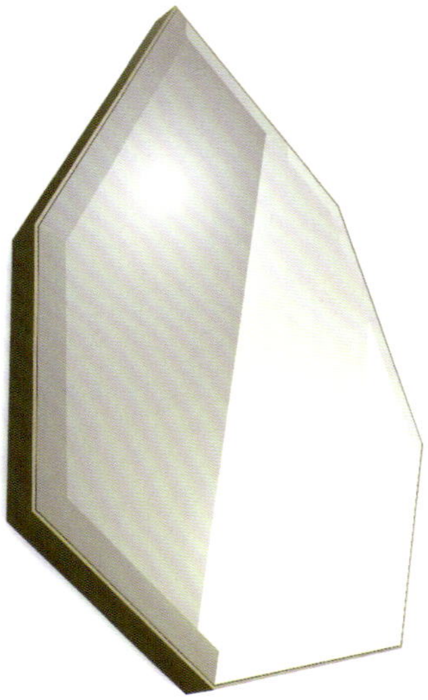

Mirror "Thétis" by JLD for Pouenat

Mural by Florence Girette

Corten steel

Curve parquet plank by Bolefloor

Wet sand-colored waxed concrete floor

PHOTO 1 / Custom-designed by Jean-Louis Deniot metal bench with woven asymmetrical straps / "Acapulco" chairs from Galerie Sentou / Deck chairs "Mistral 104" by Roda • **PHOTO 2** / Natural fiber wallpaper by Weitzner / Brushed light oak door / Custom-designed JLD fireplace in Corten steel • **PHOTOS 3 & 7** / Set of custom-designed tables (one in petrified wood, one in stained sequoia, one in bronze) / Curtains in Pedroso & Osório "Underwater" / Custom-designed JLD rug / Chandelier by Oswald Haerdtl / Painting *Collage of Bindis* by Bharti Kher / Wallpaper "Aura" by Weitzner / Vintage sofas by Vladimir Kagan in Romo linen and cotton, in Linara Driftwood, Linara Cardamon, Linara Fig, Linara Manilla, Linara Pannacotta / Bulbo vases by ImperfettoLab / Chaise longue, PK24, in rattan by Poul Kjærholm / Chair by Pierre Paulin Bisson Bruneel / Plaster lamp by Charles Trevelyan from Carpenters Workshop Gallery / Chair by Hans Wagner / Oak wall shelves • **PHOTO 4** / Sculpture made of balsa wood sticks by Xavier Veilhan / Wall behind console in large slate slab / Walls in polished cement / Chair by Pierre Jeanneret / Asymmetrical freestanding wall console by Charlotte Perriand / Coat rack, Hang it All, by Charles and Ray Eames • **PHOTOS 5 & 6** / Custom-designed JLD table in polished-and-brushed cedar / 1960s opalescent glass suspension by Gino Sarfatti / Photophore Nest by Marsia Holzer / Chairs by Michel Buffet • **PHOTO 8** / Table by Pierre Jeanneret / Mica "Plank Hanging Light" by Marsia Holzer / Kitchen appliances by Effeti Cucine Uniche / Floor in polished concrete, sand

Slate

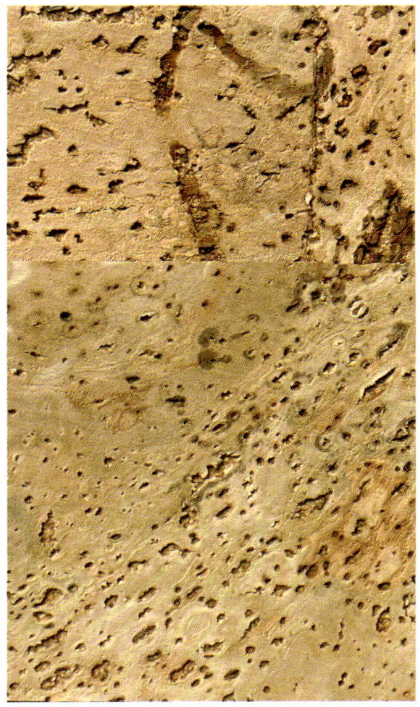

Cork wall tiles La Maison du Liège

Openwork wallpaper "Aur" by Weitzner on khaki paint base

Gradient painted sheer curtains in Underwater by Pedroso & Osório

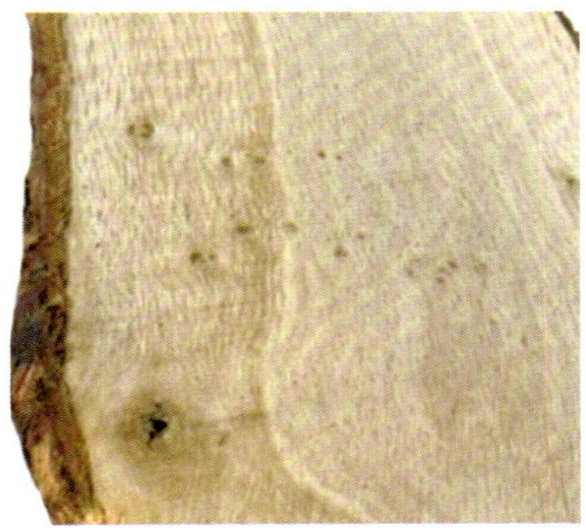

Raw wood plank

Custom-designed JLD brutalist door handle

color / Chairs by Charlotte Perriand / Curtains in Sahco's "Medusa" / Mobile by Xavier Veilhan • **PHOTO 9** / French 1950s wall lights by Maison Lunel / Kitchen island in chestnut oak • **PHOTO 10** / Bathtub Terrazzo, design Jirko Bannas, manufactured using local lauze stone / Tucker Robbins's Mountain Pine Ladder / Taps Watermark "Brooklyn" / Vases by Gilles Caffier / Custom-designed JLD mirror / Local Lauze stone back wall / Polished concrete floor by Marius Aurenti • **PHOTO 11** / Custom-designed JLD bed by Pierre Eloi Bris, sculpted out of old oak beams / Bedspread by Mark Alexander / Stilnovo lamp / Vase by Gilles Caffier / Bedside lamp by Gino Sarfatti / Custom-designed metal bedside table with a pivoting drawer / Pillows by Stark / Cork wall by La Maison du Liège / Painting by David Ratcliff / Stool by Joseph-André Motte • **PHOTO 12** / Decorative cushions by Etamine / Bedspread by Kravet / Natural fiber wall upholstery by Élitis / Vintage wall lights by Serge Mouille / Curve parquet plank by Bolefloor / One massive sequoia "plank" distressed, stained and mounted as a headboard / Fishnet curtains by NYA Nordiska / Rocking chair "Nap 082" by Roda • **PHOTO 13** / Mirror "Thétis" by JLD for Pouenat / Travertine stone / Faucets by Watermark • **PHOTO 14** / Sofa by Janus, in Nomi / Cushions by Kravet / Stool by Arts et Matières / Custom-designed JLD daybed covered in Perennials / Decorative cushions by Perennials and MyMaille / Deck chairs "Mistral 104" by Roda •

CAPRI
ITALY

In the heart of Capri, the prized resort Italian island since the time of the Roman republic, this five-year renovation transformed a former parsonage into a twelve-room vacation home that exudes understated ease and simplicity. The client's family residences already included a remarkable property in France at Saint-Jean-Cap-Ferrat, designed by Renzo Mongiardino, as well as homes in Paris, Milan, and Monaco renovated by Deniot. This sophisticated estate was the perfect opportunity for the Italian owners to go back to their Caprisian roots.

You speak of this project as a labor of love...

From the start, I knew this project would require intense love to make it happen. There was so much to be done. The house was badly renovated in the 1980s with white tile floor and plastic laminated doors, pergolas, and windows. We stripped it down until there was nothing left. Then, we had to dynamite part of the mountain to create more ceiling height. Because of the small and narrow streets in Capri, every single bit of debris from the renovation had to be evacuated on scooters one bucket at a time. The upside was that we had five years to source the perfect content, from humidity-appropriate art by Paola Pivi and Joana Vasconcelos, to iconic design pieces by Jean Royère, Jacques Adnet, Jean-Michel Frank, and Jacques Jarrige, as well as Georges Jouve, Gaetano Pesce, and Mattia Bonetti amongst others.

Photography by Stephan Julliard

The natural site plays an important role in the foundation of the house.

It's important for me to embrace and understand the local context, so my projects are not only well-grounded but also belong to their environment. Because cliffs form much of the surface of the island, all the construction follows the natural relief of the mountain. The house feels very much like the troglodyte structures you find in North Africa, where the relief of the stone informs the

layout of the construction and the interior spaces follow the natural curves of the site. When the rock face goes up, you go up a few steps, and when it descends, you go down. It's fantastic because each room is absolutely unique. You never have the same ceiling height or the same volume. The succession of these distinctive rooms creates a Medina-like compound that gives onto the internal courtyard and the multiple roof terraces.

It is one of the few houses you have done in white.

Actually, it's not white. Greece is white. Capri is never pure white. It is grège, a mix of yellow and grey. With the intensity of the summer light, the house has a warm glow that is generous and joyful. To accentuate it, I used a rough textured plaster and painted it in an oatmeal shade throughout so as to avoid the typical whitewashed walls.

Why did you look back to the island's founding Roman period?

Paying tribute to Capri during the Roman era allowed me to provide the house with a sense of legitimacy. I put antique floors throughout to replace the tiling and opted for antique oak interior

doors in the typical diamond-shaped paneled frames and custom handles inspired by Diego Giacometti. It was important to have a textured finish that was soft and sensual, so everything you touch is as considered as what you see.

To soften up the structure, I emphasized the curves of the ceiling, the arches, and the outside masonry. Instead of marble, I turned to Pompeian mosiacs to express a sense of materiality. I also used leather strips for the cabinet fronts in reference to the Roman shoe straps from Pompeii. Aged stone was cut and laid in a Roman opus pattern for all interior flooring. For the outside patios, I used antique terra-cotta bricks on the floor and old wood for the pergolas to give the patina of time. The natural flora of Capri adorns the patios with bougainvillea, adding bursts of color on the terrace that contrast with the subdued palette of the interior.

Distressed wood

Textured plaster

Irregular stone mosaic

Pale terra-cotta bricks

Leather straps

Aged opus stone

PHOTO 1 / Sculpture by Jean-Michel Othoniel / Scarred bench from Ochre • **PHOTO 2** / 1960s bone console table by Karl Springer / Pair of plaster tables lamps from Galerie Mougin / Custom-designed Jean-Louis Deniot mirror • **PHOTO 3** / Wall lights in ceramic by Georges Jouve / 1950s bamboo chair in Le Manach / 1930s plaster ceiling light • **PHOTO 4** / Institution of Culture in metal by Anya Zholud • **PHOTO 5** / Crab sculpture by Joana Vasconcelos / 1930s plaster ceiling light / Two stools as a column by Peter Lane / Cabinet by Mattia Bonetti • **PHOTO 6** / 1950s table lamp with base made from a roll used for printing patterns on textiles, custom raffia shade by Anne Sokolsky / Vintage ceramic vases • **PHOTO 7** / Pair of armchairs by Audoux Minet in Dedar and Rubelli, IDF piping / Custom-designed JLD cowhide patchwork rug by Maison Fey / Sofa by Gio Ponti in Rubelli / Decorative pillows, Rubelli / Curtains, Métaphores and Edmond Petit / Custom sofa by JLD in Romo and Pierre Frey, IDF piping / Cushions, Brunschwig, Rubelli, and Pierre Frey, IDF piping / *Medusa Adrift in the Great Pacific Garbage* by Christian Holstad / Custom-designed JLD chandelier in plaster / Coffee table in marcasite by Ado Chale from Galerie Gastou / 1950s and '60s ceramic vases from Teo Leo / Osselets stools by Jacques Jarrige from Galerie Cat-Berro / Wooden sculpture *Stone –Constructive Failures III* by Damian Ortega • **PHOTO 8** / Black bamboo chairs with pillow seats in Dedar fabric / 1940s metal table / Roman blind in horsehair by Le Crin • **PHOTO 9** / Two tables by Jacques Jarrige from Galerie

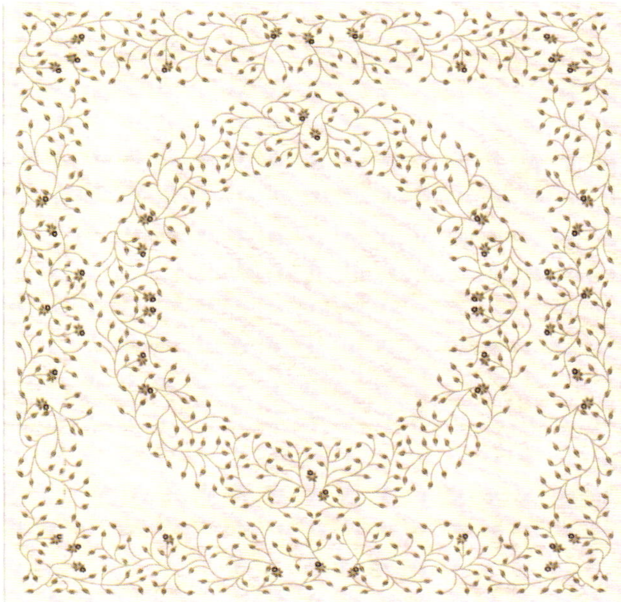

Custom-designed JLD rug

Bamboo

Braided rope

Straw

Cat-Berro / French 1940s dining chairs in horsehair by Le Crin / 1960s chandelier by Venini from Galerie Nilufar / 1950s iron candleholders from Teo Leo / Curtains, Kirk Brummel / Rug in banana leaf fiber by Rush Matters / Photography *Spanish Bath* by James Casebere • **PHOTO 10** / Rattan chairs by Vittorio Bonacina / Custom-designed JLD table in travertine and bronze / Pair of painted bronze watermelon by Oliver Babin / Indonesian ceiling light • **PHOTO 11** / Painted concrete bench / Set of cushions in Perennials / Armchair by Franco Albini / Set of three wood stools by Art et Matières / Forged-iron lantern from Galerie Teo Leo • **PHOTO 12** / Custom-designed JLD straw headboard / Tie dye pillow / Bedspread in Romo, IDF piping / *Fevrier 09* painting by Bernard Frize • **PHOTO 13** / Custom-designed JLD oak and leather desk / Nineteenth-century iron curule from Philippe Colangelo covered in pearl-green leather / Pair of vintage ceramic table lamps from Los Angeles / Photography *Boy and Girl* by Leandro Erlich • **PHOTO 14** / Shower curtains, Edmond Petit / Cabinet doors in woven leather strap / Ceiling lamp in bronze and glass by Nautic / Custom-designed JLD mirror by Garouste et Bonetti • **PHOTO 15** / Custom bed by JLD / Custom-designed JLD rug by Diurne / Silk and cotton bedspread by Alta Pampa Argentina / 1940s stone small mirror from Galerie du Passage / "Pierres Sèches" side table by Mattia Bonetti from Galerie Cat-Berro / 1970s table lamp / Ceiling lamp by Gaetano Pesce from Galerie Nilufar / Photography *One Love* by Paola Pivi •

MOSCOW
RUBLYOVKA

In the vibrant city of Moscow, this pied-à-terre for a young Russian family is located in the prestigious district of Rublyovka, home to Russian elites dating back to Peter the Great. From the start, the idea was to make the apartment feel new and playful but also well-established. The design, defined by a seemingly classical elegance, introduces a striking twist to create a sense of movement in a city known for its speed.

Conceived as an open space, the apartment can be easily modulated to create different size rooms through a system of sliding doors, which offers options and flexibility, allowing one to effortlessly personalize the space.

From the entrance, you created a striking graphic rhythm.

Yes, a kind of vortex. I have the lasting impression that Moscow never really sleeps, especially in the summer when the nights are so short. I wanted the apartment to feel young and fresh and to radiate the sense of energy that I love about the city.

Everything has been done in the most conventional manner, even though the design doesn't feel very traditional. I wanted to honor conventional handcraft techniques and translate them in a more contemporary way. In the gallery entrance, the marble pilasters have a striking black edge which gives the feeling of a portico. The walls in uneven stripes are hand-painted in a fresco technique. Because there is no natural light coming in, the more you play with graphics the more vibrant the space becomes visually.

Photography by Stephan Julliard

The system of sliding doors plays an important role in the distribution of the apartment. It's like living in a huge open loft with countless sliding doors that create wall-like partitions. Depending on the time of day, you can separate rooms to feel more private or more spacious, isolating yourself or spreading out into connecting spaces. It's very chameleon in terms of use.

Starting in the main gallery, I established a sense of symmetry with doors clad in leather rectangular nail studs and bronze door custom hardware. A pediment was added above each door to stretch the ceiling height. Instead of being purely linear, the casing extends all the way to the ceiling molding, giving a sense of more volume.

You designed many custom elements for this project.

In the salon, the radiating patterned rugs were all made-to-measure. Frequently used during the Napoleonic period, the *verre églomisé* panels in the back have a contemporary abstract landscape that shimmers at night. Opened, they give access to hidden storage and, in some cases, to secret doors that lead you to different rooms.

In the kitchen, I prefer not to have upper cabinets. Instead, I try to create full walls of cabinetry. What would have been a short backsplash suddenly becomes a stunning single slab, an abstracted art piece that is unique. It looks less like a kitchen and more like a cool bar with all functions perfectly accessible.

What to do with a small room?

If you have a small room, why not try to make it as mysterious as you can? It creates a sense of new possibility. When I initially presented the idea for the bedroom, the client was completely against it. And, to her credit, there was a lot going on: hand-painted canvas, mirrored walls, textured wallpaper, and, to top it all off, I included a black ceiling. I knew that the light would reflect on the elements and bring them together. Ironically, today it's her favorite room in the apartment.

PIRANESI

Custom-designed JLD rug by Solstys

Fabric with gold part by Sabina Fay Braxton

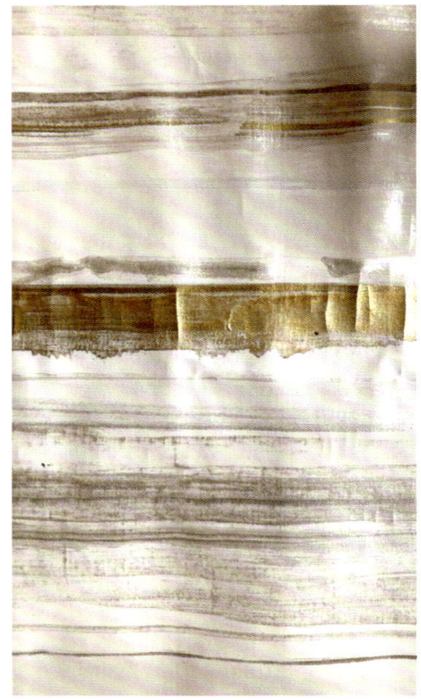

Painted stripes on canvas

Grey with black marble floor pattern

Textured silvered glass

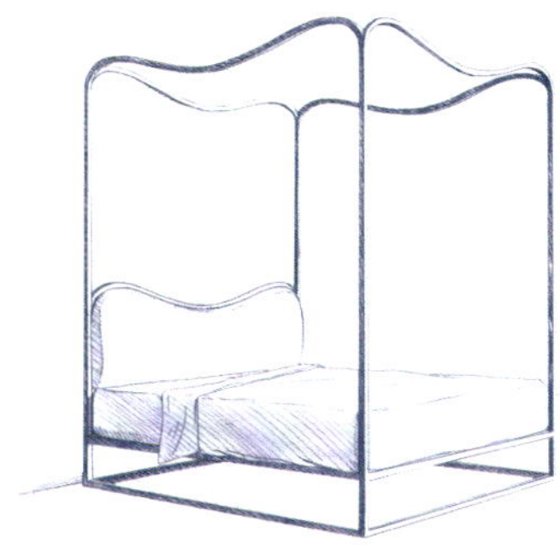

Custom-designed JLD bed

PHOTO 1 / Wall decorative paint effect by Florence Girette / Custom-designed Jean-Louis Deniot marble floor pattern • **PHOTO 2** / Side table by Pierre Counot Blandin / Custom-designed JLD curved sofa in Kvadrat and Pierre Frey / Brass coffee table by Erwam Boulloud from Galerie Glustin / Sofa by JLD for Baker in Jules et Jim and Lelièvre / Set of decorative pillows in Brochier, Pierre Frey and Sabina Fay Braxton, Houlès piping / Pair of custom-designed JLD rough rock crystal candalabra on plaster columns / Pair of 1960s candleholders by Dorothy Thorpe / Set of two marble boxes with brass trim / Two candleholders by Gilles Caffier / Glass piece by Alexa Lixfeld • **PHOTO 3** / Vintage bergère by Bruno Le Yaouanc in Rubelli, Mokuba piping / Alabaster egg lamp by Alain Ellouz • **PHOTO 4** / Pair of custom ombré curtains by Pierre Frey / Alabaster urn table lamp from Galerie Blanchetti • **PHOTO 5** / Dining table "Interference" by Hervé Van Der Straeten / Set of ten leather and cane dining chairs / Set of six vintage candlesticks / Pair of crystal chandeliers by Mathieu Lustrerie / Pair of half-moon consoles with travertine top / Concealed closet doors clad in back-painted glass by Florence Girette • **PHOTO 6** / Set of three brutalist hanging lights / Handmade ceramic vase by Karen Swami • **PHOTO 7** / Custom-designed JLD rug by Solstys / Vintage table by Roger Tibier with glass top and brass legs / Set of Art Déco vintage chairs in Ido fabric • **PHOTO 8** / Vintage Louis XVI-style desk / Desk chair by Carlyle Collective in Pierre Frey / Pair of armchairs in Créations Métaphores / Set of four wall lights "Tube" by Hervé Van Der Straten / Pair of side tables "Epines" by Hervé Van Der Straeten / Mirror "Solaire" by Hervé Van Der Straeten / Two pairs of candleholders by

Back-painted glass

Custom-designed JLD rug by Solstys

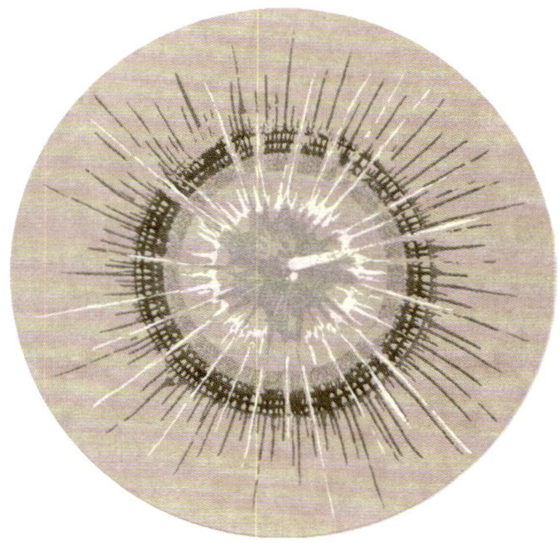

Custom-designed JLD rug by Solstys

Dark grey stained Versailles oak wood floor

Back-painted glass

Ivar Ålenius Björk for Ystad / Sofa by Amy Somerville in Pierre Frey, pillows in Jim Thompson and Designers Guild / Set of decorative pillows in Manuel Canovas, Houlès piping / Painted canvas by Florence Girette on walls and ceiling • **PHOTO 9** / Custom-designed JLD rug by Solstys / Wallpaper for ceiling by Annie Pate / Wallpaper by Arte / Curtains in Pasaya fabric / Custom-designed JLD headboard in Le Manach / Bedcover in Glant fabric / Custom-designed JLD nightstands / Vintage pair of Murano table lamps, lampshades by Anne Sokolsky • **PHOTO 10** / Custom-designed JLD rug by Solstys / Wallpaper for ceiling and walls by Annie Paté / Painted canvas by Florence Girette on the headboard wall / Custom-designed JLD brass bed structure with headboard in Scion fabric / Bedcover in Pierre Frey fabric / Pair of cushions in Pierre Frey, and Houlès piping / Pair of custom-designed JLD nightstand lamps with glass pieces / Mirror "Facette" by Hervé Van Der Straeten / Armchair upholstered in Sahco • **PHOTO 11** / Custom-designed JLD vanities / Set of four wall lights by Circa Lighting • **PHOTO 12** / Gold-painted curtains by Sabina Fay Braxton / Custom-designed JLD rug by Solstys / Hand-painted silk and embroidered wallpaper by Fromental / Custom-designed JLD headboard in Métaphores, Houlès and Mokuba piping / Bedspread in Lauren Hwang fabric / Pair of decorative pillows by Sabina Fay Braxton / Pair of wall lights by Bert Franck / Mirror "Brindilles" by Hervé Van Der Straeten / Pair of custom-designed JLD nightstands / Pair of custom-designed JLD stools in Lauren Hwang fabric •

NEW DELHI
MONAPESY MANOR

Originally a field of wheat with a small pond and a dozen centennial trees in the outskirts of New Delhi, Deniot's first estate built from the ground up is today a palatial splendor. Dating from nearly twenty years ago, this construction project turned out to be a successful leap of faith for both the designer and the client, based on mutual trust and constructed thanks to the technical ingenuity and distinctive skill of India's gifted craftsmen.

India is a special place for you.

I've lived many firsts in India. To begin with, this is the first house I built. I was twenty-eight when I started drawing it and two years later construction began. In all, the property took five years to build and is sourced from only local artisans and resources, 100 percent a product of India.

It has been almost twenty years since you built this home.

Even though I really love the challenge of finding solutions in a pre-existing structure, it's very different building a house from scratch than renovating an existing space. When you build, it's fantastic because everything comes together in a single narrative. There's a unique point of view, with no limitations and with full responsibility for the entire structure. You have to trust the journey and in this case it certainly was unforgettable. For me, it was definitely the first of everything!

This construction was a unique experience of on-site trial and error.

I was so young in the process. I was doing sample moldings on every facade to physically try out each pattern. Now, I can design from a distance an absolute perfect-size molding. But at that time I needed to try it out on-site with the Indian artisan on his bamboo scaffolding and the Indian women in saris carrying the cement on their heads, very much like a century ago. It was an incredible experience.

Photography by Stephan Julliard

Right: Photography by Richard Powers

There is something extremely rewarding about going back to the basics.

What I love about India is you can give me a pile of plaster, wood, cement, and marble and two hundred artisans and that's all I need. The level of craftsmanship is so high and so accessible that the clients never talk costs because they know I embrace the local materials. I bring the design. They hire two hundred artisans, and suddenly the project allows you to feed two hundred families for five years while the construction is being built.

How did you envision the house?

Initially, the clients showed me a picture of Pablo Picasso's home, Villa California, in the South of France. But it didn't make sense to design a French villa in India. Instead, I worked around neoclassical references during the British colonial period and took inspiration from the famed English architect Edwin Lutyens, who designed and built New Delhi in the early twentieth century. In the process, the house tripled in size, but not because we needed more rooms. It was because I needed the rooms to be more spacious.

THE ROYAL PALACE

Drawing its inspiration from classical antiquity, the neoclassicism movement had a very strong impact on you.

For me, it's the base vocabulary. I am particularly interested by the Empire style, which had its cultural center in Paris during the Napoleonic era in the early nineteenth century. This project presented me with the rare opportunity and perfect outlet to try out my designs full-scale in this very academic style that so fascinated me at the time.

Did these elements serve as a template for your stylistic vocabulary?

It's a template, yes, but the only variation of its kind. This project allowed me to express every aspect of neoclassicism that interested me. The truth is I had nothing else to say after that. I said it all with this single project, which allowed me to move on. I used it more as a template of how to work on an international scale while collaborating locally. The process allowed me to learn flexibility and to adapt to the construction cultures of different countries.

Looking back, is there anything you would have changed had you done the house today?

The irony is there was recently a fire on the second floor of the house, and thankfully it was only structural. I traveled to India for two days, and reordered everything. I actually corrected the color tuning from the initial construction, which was invisible to anyone but me. The second version is more fine-tuned than the first but the overall design of the house is as pertinent today as when it was built nearly two decades ago.

Toys for Boys
INDIA

Limestone stucco

Painted wooden trellis on mirror

Black-and-white Indian marble

Gold leaf on woodwork

Gold leaf on cornice and paneling

Custom-designed JLD cross-pattern mirror frame

PHOTO 1 / Wicker-and-teak furniture in Brunschwig & Fils outdoor fabrics / Indonesian umbrellas • **PHOTO 2** / Nineteenth-century set of lanterns / Armand Albert Rateau-inspired armchairs manufactured in Mumbai / Louis XVI–style wall lights / Custom-designed Jean-Louis Deniot hammered-brass urn / Custom-designed JLD Pompeian-style console with ebony-stained teak / Marble obelisk table lamps / Custom-designed JLD forged-iron mirror / Faux-stone stucco over plaster paneling by JLD / Curtains in linen from local market, Houlès piping / Flooring Indian white marble mixed with Indian black marble • **PHOTO 3** / Empire-style table stained in brown and ebony accents with marble top matching the identical floor pattern / Hanging lights with Venetian glass bubbles / Railing inspired by a French eighteenth-century railing / Bench stained in a glossy ebony finish / Mirror in carved wood with a gold leaf finish / 38-foot-high ceiling all custom designed by JLD • **PHOTO 4** / Custom-designed JLD cabinet in black-and-ivory lacquer finish / Two artworks in acrylic on canvas by Sanjeev Varma • **PHOTO 5** / Custom-designed JLD "Coin de feu" sofas in Seasons fabric / Table with lacquered brass and black opaline top by Collection Pierre / Set of cushions in Seasons fabric / Stool in Pierre Frey velvet fabric / Coffee table by Collection Pierre / Fireplace and Directoire-style mirror. All custom designed by JLD • **PHOTO 6** / Stool in Pierre Frey velvet fabric / Chandelier from 1stDibs / Side table inspired by Pompeian-period piece / Paneling with gold leaf, ivory and pearl gray / Pair of cabinets clad with black mother-of-pearl / Rug in the André Arbus style typical of the French 1940s, all custom designed by JLD • **PHOTO 7** / Custom-designed JLD ottoman in Romo velvet / Custom-designed JLD hammered-brass urn • **PHOTO 8** / Lacquered-oak armchairs in Edmond Petit fabric / 1940s-style table with limestone-and-black-marble top / Distressed copper chandelier. All custom designed by JLD • **PHOTO 10** / Louis XVI-style sofas / 1930s Ruhlmann-style lamps manufactured

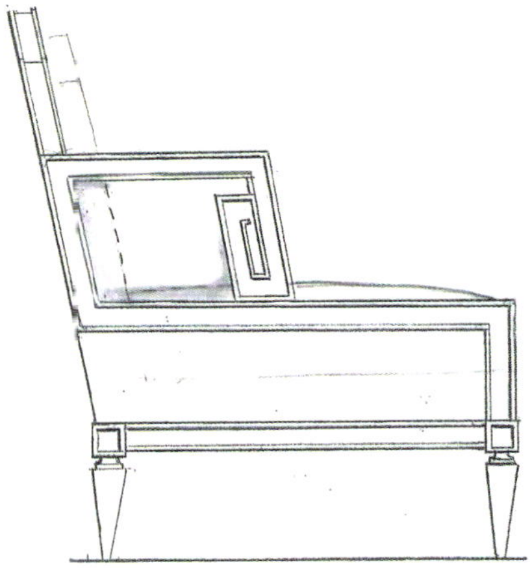

Custom-designed JLD Greek key-style sofa

Embroidered-and-hand-painted silk border

Detailed paint work

Jute rug from India

Black mother-of-pearl

in India / Terra-cotta vase manufactured in India • **PHOTO 11** / Custom-designed JLD distressed mirror behind trellis / Jute rug manufactured in South India / Flooring inspired by the Château de Groussay in local Indian marble designed by JLD • **PHOTO 12** / Alabaster celling light, carved-wood gilded wall lights, 1940s-style iron console, all manufactured in India • **PHOTO 13** / Klismos chair, black high-gloss finish / Custom-designed JLD 25-foot-long neoclassical-style table / Directoire-style chandeliers / Door to main living room, antique mirror insert and hand-painted based on a JLD design / Bronze wall lights / Empire-style paneling designed by JLD with various shades of terra-cotta finishes / Custom-designed JLD "Dragon Wings" patterned ceiling with a mix of local paints / Custom-designed JLD rug in a mix of neoclassical and bindi-style dots • **PHOTO 14** / Divan upholstered with Seasons fabric / Custom-designed JLD cocktail table in gold leaf and black marble top / Custom-designed JLD chair upholstered in cowskin, decorative pillow in suede / Hand-painted border and trim on ceiling and doors / Wallpaper by Au Fil des Couleurs / Curtain borders embroidered by Jean François Lesage / Black and white Indian marble flooring • **PHOTO 15** / Canopy in black semi-gloss ebony-stained mahogany / Hanging light in brass with an antique finish and frosted glass / TV ottoman covered in Seasons fabric, Mokuba piping / Pair of wood armchairs upholstered in Season / Mirror inspired by a Line Vautrin model / Daybed inspired by André Arbus / Bone-clad side table / Sconces in two-tone bronze / Paneling inspired by Louis Sue and André Mare, in in mahogany with black-stained ebony inserts and gold-leaf accents / Rug manufactured in India, inspired by André Arbus. All custom designed JLD •

BANGKOK
SUKHUMVIT ROAD

Referred to as the "Venice of the East," Bangkok is an expansive metropolis where speed and vitality collide. In the dynamic urban hub of Sukhumvit, an impressive contemporary tower provides spectacular 360 degree views of the bustling city. Regrouping the top three floors of this modern skyscraper, the striking apartment is designed for generous entertaining and living.

You treated the project as if it were a boat.

From the beginning, this apartment reminded me of a big ship at the top of a building. On three full floors you are completely surrounded by windows. All the casings are steel blades reminiscent of those found on boats. Every corridor you walk through and every window casing is framed with distressed steel to enhance a cleaner and sharper overall effect.

Why did you begin by creating an atrium?

I needed to vertically connect the three floors and also bring in natural light. To resolve these challenges, I created a spacious atrium anchored by an intricate transparent staircase. A visually unifying statement, the staircase needed to be sharp, light, and thin, so I used glass and metal to achieve a delicate silhouette. Between the silver and gold elements, I employed a matte champagne finish to give warmth and luminosity like a ray of light. For the backdrop, I commissioned the French artists Les Farfelu Farfardets to do a bas-relief in papier-mâché, creating an abstract three-dimensional city skyline that sweeps the eyes upward.

To give a more mineral quality, the walls are treated with marble powder and are colored in degradé from white to black; this is reversed on the second floor, generating a completely different result.

Photography by Stephan Julliard

STEVE McCURRY ANIMALS

When you have 18,000 square feet on three floors, how do you think about the flow of the apartment?

It is very important to make sure the owners do not need to live on multiple levels the whole time because they would get tired of it. We placed all the main functions on one level. Entertainment and guest rooms on the second level, and then outdoor dining, a pool, a winter garden, and terrace on

the third level. Each living space takes into consideration the positions of the sunrise and sunsets to provide appropriate seating areas. With the passing seasons, the owners can favor certain levels more than others.

With only three bedrooms, it is truly a reception apartment.

It was definitely designed to receive a lot of people comfortably. There's an entire area on the second level dedicated to entertainment, including a 3,000-square-foot party room with an alabaster floor, a backlit bar entirely open to the skyline, and a nearly 10-foot-long aquarium where everything is white, from the fish to the corals and rocks, to the back paneling.

There is even a private gold grotto that opens at the flip of a switch.

Initially it was supposed to be a bar, inspired by "One Night in Bangkok" and James Bond 007. But the lady of the house said that five bars was enough. So we revised the layout and made it into a contemplation room. All the lighting comes from the baseboard for maximum comfort. In a gold *dégradé*, it starts as a dark bronze on the floor level. Also, the custom rug makes reference to the elements of smoke and wind.

You've added an element of playfulness with the secret doors...

I love it because it is very childish. It's marvelous when you have a pivoting mirror or an open armoire that allows you to secretly access another room. When possible, I always try to create playful moments. But there is also a more pragmatic reason. Thailand is one of those countries that is highly staffed. When you live in an apartment with such a large housekeeping team, it is important to create areas of real privacy.

On the top floor, the apartment has its own helipad.

Yes, and it structurally covers the pool below. To take advantage of the physical constraint, I decided to go full-on eighteenth-century France and create a grotto-like cave for the pool area. In Bangkok, the sun is so bright and the heat is so intense that an enclosed pool actually makes much more sense and exudes wonder and freshness. There is even a waterfall and multiple fountains throughout to evoke a playful lagoon.

AIS
5G
เร็วที่สุด

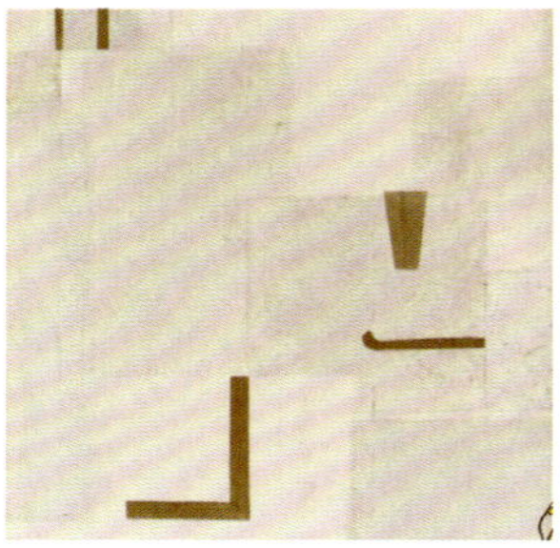

Painted screen by Florence Girette

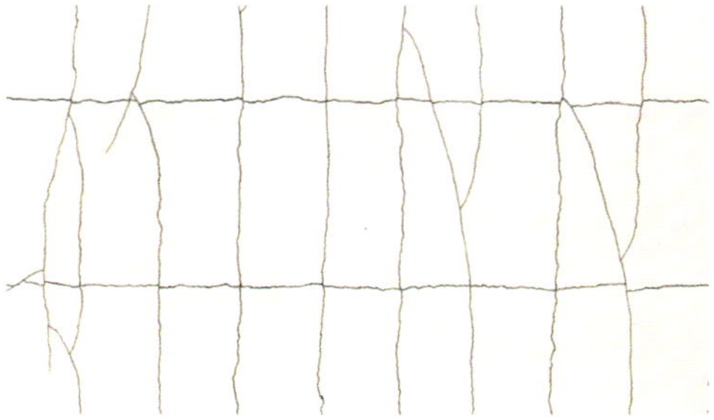

Faux-crackled ivory

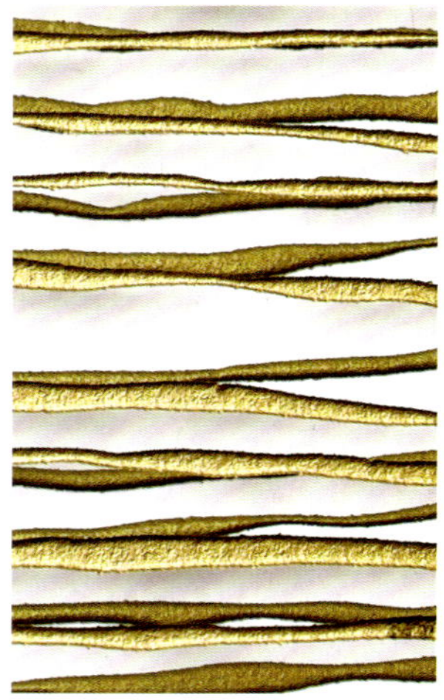

Engraved gold steps

Papier-mâché low relief by Les Farfelu Farfadets

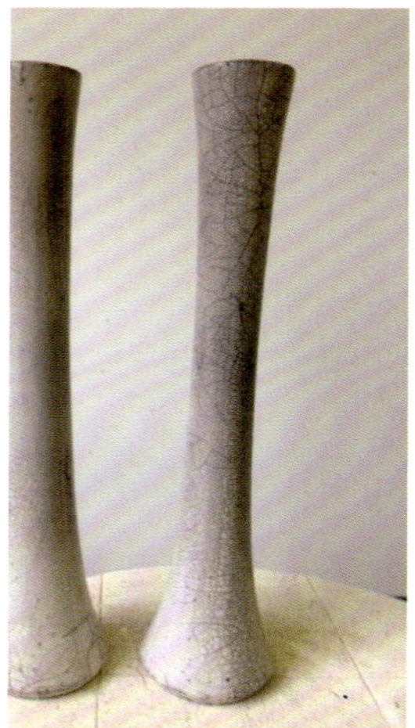

Raku ceramic JLD design

Custom-designed JLD sofa

PHOTO 1 / Low-relief papier-mâché by Les Farfelu Farfadets Paris / Ombré wall stucco by Atelier du Mur / Stairs in engraved-glass gold finish • **PHOTO 2** / Custom-designed Jean-Louis Deniot sofa in Boussac / Decorative pillows in Dédar and Lelièvre, Houlès piping / Marble and cast brass coffee table by Vincenzo de Cotiis / Pair of armchairs in Manuel Canovas and Sanderson / Pair of enameled lava side tables by Christophe Delcourt / Custom-designed JLD black-iron and gold-leaf side table / Custom-designed JLD antique hammered-brass pedestal / Candlesticks and three vases by Alexander Lamont / Ceramic art by Bathma Kaew-Ngok / Flower styling by Naomi Daimaru • **PHOTO 3** / Hand-cast scagliola coffee table by McCollin Bryan • **PHOTO 4** / Custom-designed JLD rug by Solstys / Pair of armchairs by Arflex in Karine Sajo / Pair of cast-iron floor lamps by JLD for Marc de Berny / Pair of stools from Arflex by Gaston y Daniela / White marble and black tiles side table by Porcelain Bear / Pair of "Telemaque" armchairs designed by JLD for Pouenat in Casamance / Sofa by Baxter in Nobilis / Set of decorative pillows in Dedar, Houlès piping / Painted electric screen by Florence Girette / Custom-designed JLD set of metallic flowers / Candlesticks by Alexander Lamont / Lamps by Mathilde Pénicaud / Flower styling by Naomi Daimaru • **PHOTO 5** / Custom-designed JLD bench in Rubelli / Abstract art by Anonymous • **PHOTO 6** / Custom-designed JLD rug by Solstys / Distressed gold-leaf ceiling / Dining table by Piet Hein Eek / Pair of bronze and clear glass chandeliers by Roll & Hill / Dining chairs by Kelly Wearstler in Edmond Petit and Pierre Frey / Custom-designed JLD mirror in two-tone shagreen / Vases by Alexander Lamont / Flower styling by Naomi Daimaru • **PHOTO 7** / Ombré-lacquered walls / Custom-designed JLD door pull with textured wallpaper insert "Caiman" by Casmance / Floor lamp by Atelier Areti • **PHOTO 8** / Custom-designed JLD rug by Solstys / Custom-designed JLD sofa in Romo / Set of decorative pillows in Pierre Frey and Création Baumann, Houlès piping / Pair of wooden side tables by Anna Karlin / Custom-

Ombré stucco by Atelier du Mur

Vibrant gold leaf with ombré base

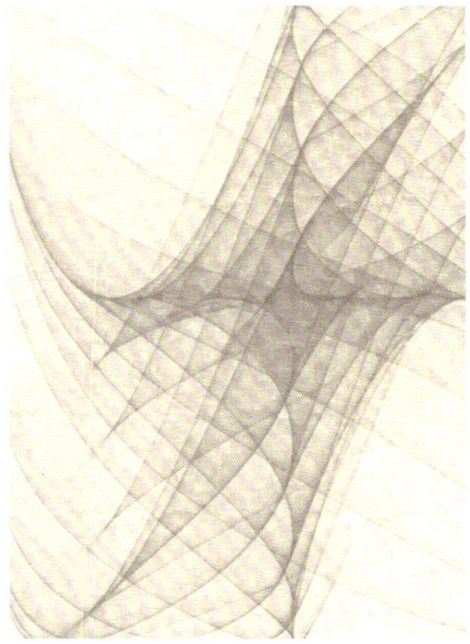

Custom-designed JLD rug manufactured by Solstys

Cement grotto wall finish

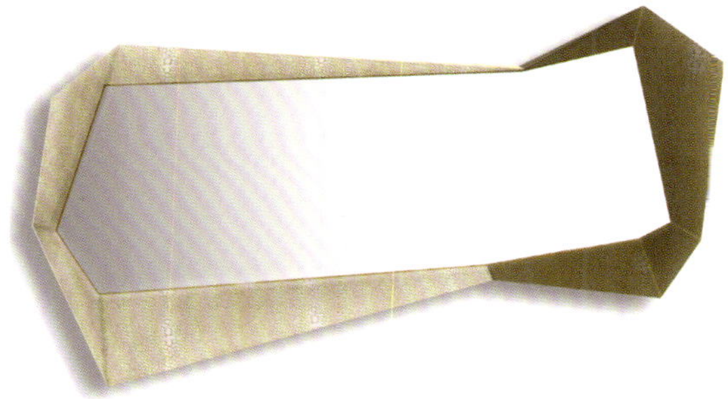

Custom-designed JLD shagreen mirror

designed JLD marble and antique brass coffee table / Pair of armchairs by Mark de Berny in Rubelli / Candlesticks by Saccal Design House / Vases by Alexander Lamont / Flower styling by Naomi Daimaru • **PHOTO 9** / Custom-designed JLD rug by Solstys / Wall upholstery in Casamance / Bed designed by JLD for Baker in Casamance / Set of decorative pillows in Romo / Pair of lacquered bedside tables by Hervé Van der Straeten / Pair of gold ceiling lights by Hind Rabii / Custom-designed JLD benches with gold metal base in Casamance / Custom-designed JLD gypse-clad chest of drawers / Flower styling by Naomi Daimaru • **PHOTO 10** / Kalakata marble • **PHOTO 11** / Pair of custom-designed JLD mirrors in hammered nickel silver / Two pairs of steel, aluminium and glass ceiling lights by Roll & Hill • **PHOTO 12** / Pair of wall lights by Bomma / Pair of curtains in Sahco / Custom-designed JLD bench for Baker • **PHOTOS 13, 14, 15 & 16** / Custom-designed JLD rug by Solstys / Custom-designed JLD oak bed frame by Kelly Wearstler for Lee Jofa / Bedspread in Métaphores / Decorative pillows in Lelièvre, Houlès piping / Pair of lime black oak bedside tables by Julian Chichester / Pair of custom-designed JLD ceramic bedside table lamps, lampshade by Anne Sokolsky / Daybed by Made by the Morgans in Romo / Armchair by PLEASE WAIT to be SEATED in Lelièvre / Ivory gloss wood and antique-bronze metal side table by Baker / Brushed-brass-and-glass floor lamp by Roche Bobois / Mirror by Hervé Van Der Straeten / Pair of curtains in Lelièvre • **PHOTO 17** / Rattan sofa and armchair by Sika / Decorative pillows in Link / Coffee table by Tribu / Vases by Alexander Lamont / Flower styling by Naomi Daimaru • **PHOTO 18** / Pair of rattan chairs by Sika / Dining table by Ames / Vases by Alexander Lamont / Flower styling by Naomi Daimaru • **PHOTO 19** / Pair of armchairs by Gae Aulenti, re-edition by Exteta / Side table by Ce London •

TANGIER
MOROCCO

On the Moroccan coast where the Mediterranean Sea meets the Atlantic Ocean, Tangier is a port town, a bridge between Europe and Africa. Strategically located on the strait of Gibraltar, Tangier is less than ten miles away from the Spanish coast. It is said that you go to Marrakech to be seen and to Tangier to stay under the radar. The antidote to his many obligations, it is here where Jean-Louis is truly himself, where he can recharge on his own terms and find the serenity to fuel his creative inspiration.

Your home in Tangier is an ode to nature.

It's as if it were an outdoor palace of sorts! It's on the scale of one, but it's created only by the lush vegetation. The Garden is phenomenal and it still has not reached maturity. The towering palm trees are like gigantic columns and the umbrella pines act as large arches to create a cathedral-like effect. Yes, it's a tribute to nature, very much alive and ever-changing, demanding adaptability and a very flexible plan.

What did you discover with this property?

Thanks to this marvelous place, I finally discovered and embraced the elements of nature and for the first time worked on the landscape and outdoor planning of the house that I have been perfecting for the last nine years. It's like the garden of Eden with a collection of palm trees and fantastic umbrella pines, the roses, the jasmine. It's the idyllic Mediterranean garden. I love it here because for once it's not about the interiors. It's all about the exteriors!

It's also a place of great joy...

The whole point of a unique space like this is to share it with others and create moments that celebrate life. In Tangier, there is a grand tradition of giving fun and entertaining parties. I am captivated by friends from all nationalities and age groups. Tangier represents everything I love about the rest of the world in a single location.

Photography by Anour Akrouh. Opposite photography by Peter Rodger

How has Tangier inspired you?

I finally found my tribe with whom I feel extremely comfortable to be totally myself. It's the place where I can be the most relaxed and enjoy precious times with my partner, William. Instead of seeking uniformity, it's a place that embraces diversity with an open heart and mind. That's what I find so inspiring.

Tangier has hosted many renowned and creative people, the likes of Pierre Bergé and Yves Saint Laurent, Francis Bacon, Marc Chagall, Henri Matisse, Paul Bowles, Allen Ginsburg, and Jack Kerouac ...

Traditionally, there has always been an active artistic community of multigenerational writers, painters, decorators, and creatives in general infusing the city with a mixture of culture and aesthetics.

I love the fact it has still remained untouched. It's like being in a time capsule that is oriented toward the future. I'm embracing the transformation that has begun, and I feel like I'm participating in the process with my own home. It feels like the land of opportunities.

You are always thinking about the future...

I'm not here to give you what you wish for now. My challenge is to make you discover your taste for the next fifteen to twenty years. And that's what keeps me and my clients excited. They require tremendous energy and attention, dedication, and passion. I receive messages from them years later when they are still discovering design elements in their homes, that's when they realize our attention to detail. I perform on a job for a few years, but someone will live in that space for dozens of years afterwards.

What have you learned?

I learn every day. I am always trying to improve and tweak, because we're still testing every single thing on every single site. We are always fine-tuning, perfecting, and looking to push further technically and aesthetically, always guided by the notion of excellence and harmony.

When you graduated from the prestigious École Camondo in Paris, what was your dream?

As a 25-year-old graduate, my dream was to land a project where I could demolish everything and then reconstruct the layout to fit my vision. It was the idea of being able to build, to construct. Today, the scale has changed, but I still take it as the same exercise even if certain developments are 100,000 square feet in scope.

I'm often asked which is my favorite project. I don't have one that stands out because all are my favorites in very different ways, but one thing they all have in common is that they are equally loved.

I dedicate this book to my great design and management team in Paris. I am extremely proud of our continuous achievements together and am forever thankful.

I would like to thank my partner, William, my sister, Virginie, and my parents for their unconditional love and support.

I would like to address my warmest thanks to Pamela Golbin. Our great friendship, which has spanned for over twenty years, is translated in these pages. Thank you for your trust, dedication, and excellence.

I extend my special thanks to Charles Miers, Ellen Nidy, Paul McKevitt, and Agnès Forcade for their invaluable work and involvement.

Special thanks to my dear friend, Diane Dorian Saeks, who initiated me to the process of making a great book. Thank you for your 20 years of complicity and shared passion for great interiors.

I would like to express my gratitude to all my clients, with whom I share the same interest for life, beauty and excellence, and thanks to whom everything becomes possible.

Thanks to the photographers, who are an intense pleasure to work with and who capture all of this hard work on film. To all the magazines, editors, journalists, and bloggers for their continuous support.

A special thanks to the artists and artisans, contractors and manufacturers, suppliers and local management teams for helping me to embody and achieve my design vision.

And, I would like to extend my special thanks to all the readers. Thank you for sharing this fantastic journey with us. I hope you enjoyed it and had as much of a blast as we did in creating this book for You!

Merci!

First published in the United States of America in 2022 by
Rizzoli International Publications, Inc.
300 Park Avenue South
New York, NY 10010
www.rizzoliusa.com

Publisher: Charles Miers
Editor: Ellen Nidy
Design: Paul McKevitt, SubtitleNY
Production Manager: Colin Hough Trapp
Managing Editor: Lynn Scrabis

Printed in China

2022 2023 2024 2025 2026 / 10 9 8 7 6 5 4 3 2 1

ISBN: 978-0-8478-7215-2
Library of Congress Control Number: 2022937196

Visit us online:
Facebook.com / RizzoliNewYork
instagram.com/rizzolibooks
twitter.com/Rizzoli_Books
pinterest.com/rizzolibooks
youtube.com/user/RizzoliNY
issuu.com/rizzoli